Wakefield Press

# The People's Poet Transformed

**Also by Geoff Goodfellow**

*No Collars No Cuffs*
*Bow Tie & Tails*
*No Ticket No Start: poetry from the building sites*
*Triggers: turning experiences into poetry*
*Triggers: the video*
*The Sex Poems Unleashed*
*Semi Madness: voices from Semaphore*
*Love is Cruel*
*Love is Cruel: spoken word + music CD*
*Poems for a Dead Father*
*Punch On Punch Off: poems for the employed, unemployed and under-employed*
*Waltzing with Jack Dancer: a slow dance with cancer*
*Opening the Windows to Catch the Sea Breeze: selected poems 1983–2011*

**Study Notes to the following poems are available:**

Poem for Annie – *Triggers* pp. 89–102
Don't Call Me Lad – *Triggers* pp. 73–86

**Online study guides for the following poems are available:**

**Visit www.geoffgoodfellow.com**

An Uncertain Future – *Waltzing with Jack Dancer* Study Guide
Maybe – *Waltzing with Jack Dancer* Study Guide
The Colour Blue – *Poems for a Dead Father* Study Guide
Miles Away – *Poems for a Dead Father* Study Guide
The Seventh Doctor – *Waltzing with Jack Dancer* Study Guide

**Geoff can be seen reading 'Hamming It Up' on YouTube**

# The People's Poet Transformed

**Geoff Goodfellow**

**Rebecca Bond**

Wakefield Press
16 Rose Street
Mile End
South Australia 5031
www.wakefieldpress.com.au

First published 2018



Designed by Liz Nicholson, designBITE
Typeset by Michael Deves, Wakefield Press
Photo of Geoff Goodfellow by Simon Cecere
Photo of Rebecca Bond by Festival Photography

ISBN 978 1 74305 575 5

A catalogue record for this book is available from the National Library of Australia

Wakefield Press thanks Coriole Vineyards for continued support

# Contents

# Acknowledgements

The front cover artwork features *The People's Poet* mixed media on canvas by Jan Shone, Largs Bay, South Australia. This painting is held in the private collection of David and Jacqui Weir, Semaphore, South Australia.

Geoff Goodfellow's poems contained within this book can be found in *Opening the Windows to Catch the Sea Breeze: selected poems 1983–2011* (Wakefield Press 2014).

His two stories 'Hamming It Up' and 'What Harry Taught Me' will appear in a forthcoming collection of poems and short stories from Wakefield Press.

'What Harry Taught Me' was first published in *Antipodes*, Vol. 30, No. 1, 2016, Wayne State University Press, USA.

Geoff Goodfellow would like to acknowledge Trish Brock for her invaluable editorial advice and support during the preparation of this manuscript.

The authors would also like to thank Tracey Dorian for her guidance, enthusiasm and encouragement. Their thanks, too, are extended to Michael Bollen for his wise feedback and generous support.

Rebecca Bond would like to thank her colleagues at Sacred Heart College, who have provided invaluable support and feedback for this project in among their own planning, preparing and marking. In particular she would like to acknowledge John Kelly, who has been a wonderful sounding board throughout the process.

**Geoff Goodfellow** has been writing and publishing poetry and short prose for over thirty years. He has performed his poetry at schools, colleges, universities, building and construction sites, factories, rock concerts, literary festivals and a myriad of other places. He has travelled extensively in Canada, the United States, Cuba, China, Europe and the United Kingdom, performing at International Literary Festivals, universities, jails, youth detention centres and various cultural institutions.

Translations of his poems have appeared in Mandarin, Greek, Italian and Spanish.

He is represented in *The Penguin Anthology of Australian Poetry* edited by John Kinsella (2009), *Two Centuries of Australian Poetry* edited by Mark O'Connor (Oxford 1988, 2007), *The Best Australian Poetry 2009* (UQP), and *The Best Australian Poems 2011, 2012, 2014 & 2015* (Black Inc.).

His poems have been transformed into songs by Hunters & Collectors frontman Mark Seymour, as well as by Stephen Cronin, Head of Composition, Queensland Conservatorium of Music. A dance performance was choreographed by Caroline Lawson based around his poem 'Reminders' and staged in December 2000 at the Space Theatre at the Adelaide Festival Centre.

Geoff tours regularly, performing and conducting classes and workshops.

He lives close to the sea in Semaphore, South Australia.

Enquiries can be directed to **poetforhire@picknowl.com.au**

**Rebecca Bond** is a middle and senior school English teacher with fifteen years' experience. She has taught in the APY Lands, various schools and colleges throughout Adelaide, South Australia, and in London, UK.

In recent years she has specialised in an all-boys' context and has facilitated learning programs for students who have low literacy skills. Her passion is to create learning opportunities that are engaging, meaningful and relevant for all students in the English classroom.

She enjoys working collaboratively to support teachers with curriculum development and has led curriculum mapping in key learning teams. In 2012 and 2017 she presented a workshop at the South Australian English Teachers Association Annual Conference.

Rebecca lives in Brighton, South Australia and currently teaches at Sacred Heart College, Somerton Park. She is available for PD sessions and curriculum support with teaching staff for a variety of school contexts.

Enquiries can be directed to **beccbond@gmail.com**

# The Transformation Task

Rebecca Bond

In 2016 I found myself teaching senior English at Sacred Heart College, Somerton Park after many years teaching predominantly in a middle school setting. The faculty were transitioning the changes in line with the new Australian Curriculum, which included the development of the Transformation Task. I was excited by the scope for choice and creativity that the Transformation Task offered.

At the time, South Australian poet Geoff Goodfellow had begun his annual three weeks' residency at the college. I was immediately drawn to how easily his work leant itself to the Transformation Task for senior English students. I also had the added bonus of having him in my classroom talking with students about his writing process and the stories behind the poems he performed for them, an invaluable resource for both myself and my students. This book is the result of a wonderful classroom partnership, and a shared passion for the power of literature in shaping and changing the way people view and engage with the world.

The idea of transformation has become a fundamental characteristic of Australian popular culture. A growing number of lifestyle programs and reality TV shows demonstrate our fascination with what we can do to make ourselves look and feel better. The essence of these shows is 'making over', whether it be house, body, food, relationships or even pets.

Take, for example, one of the many home renovation shows currently on free to air television: over the course of a season, while the basic structure or shell of the house remains, the rooms and facades are transformed into something completely new. These home renovation shows are as much about the process as they are about the final product. Episodes highlight the choices made at each step of the renovation, paying particular attention to the things that are worthy of keeping intact while finding new ways to reinvent the space. The culmination is the final reveal, and the success of the transformation lies in how well the contestants were able to maintain the original integrity of the house while bringing a fresh new look overall. Although the end product seems to have little resemblance to the original, the old charm and appeal remain for the owners who knew the house well before it was transformed. It's a fabulous analogy to use with students approaching the Transformation Task.

The Transformation Task allows students to deepen their understanding of the core text while strengthening the student's understanding of text genres. Students engage with a published text by understanding the context in which the text was created, the choices the author has made, and how they are positioned as a reader in relation to the ideas presented in the text. Usually the context and motivations of a particular text are based on researching the time, place and circumstances in which the text was created. *The People's Poet Transformed* provides teachers and students with a rare opportunity to gain an insight about the creation of the text directly from the author, which enables a more authentic transformation of the original work.

Once the context is identified, the Transformation Task requires students to transform the existing text. The transformation must involve a significant alteration to an element of the original work. Both the original and the transformed text can be of any genre, making the Transformation Task broader than straight adaptation as in the films *Romeo and Juliet* or *To Kill a Mockingbird*. Well-known transformations, such as *Emma* into *Clueless* or *Hamlet* into *The Lion King*, have altered the genre and the intended audience, as well as the meaning of the original texts.

The Transformation Task is designed to enable students to demonstrate their understanding of the structure, purpose, audience, context and stylistic features of an original text. Students choose to maintain certain elements from the original text that become the 'springboard' for their new text. Through the transformation process they demonstrate both how the original text created meaning and how this meaning can be altered for a new audience, purpose or context. The Writer's Statement aspect of the Transformation Task allows students to analyse and evaluate the relationship between the original text and the transformed text they have created.

In English classrooms it is important to encourage students to write and create texts that have meaning for them. After all, the study of English is about the fundamental ways in which we communicate and interact with others and our world. The Transformation Task is a wonderful opportunity for students to be creative, engage with language and develop skills to communicate effectively in a range of contexts and audiences.

# How to Use this Textbook

## *For teachers:*

Geoff Goodfellow is well known as 'The People's Poet'. His raw and honest insights into an array of human experiences and emotions make his work easily accessible to the ordinary person. This accessibility makes his poetry and short stories excellent springboard texts for senior English Transformation Tasks as set out in the new Australian National Curriculum.

*The People's Poet Transformed* has been designed for use by teachers and students alike. It uses a selection of Geoff's previously published poems along with two short stories from a forthcoming collection of creative non-fiction. A 'context statement' preceding each of Geoff's texts provides students with a unique insight into the original intention for the text.

Following each of Geoff's poems I have designed a set of **Transformation Tasks** to focus on a central theme from the springboard text and incorporate a range of text types for students to engage with. Some of these tasks also provide links with the critical perspectives theory that students begin to explore in Stages 1 and 2. My hope is that the ideas provided will inspire your own ideas, and those of your students. The possibilities for how these texts can be transformed are endless!

The **Writer's Statement** section of the book includes Geoff's transformation of his original poem 'Don't Call Me Lad' into the new poem 'Don't Look So Glum'. While the text type remains the same (poem) the transformation is in the narrative perspective. A sample Writer's Statement follows, demonstrating required structure and content for this task.

The final chapter provides support materials to assist students with writing in a variety of genres. There is an index of the text types used in the sets of Transformation Tasks for easy reference if your focus is on a particular genre.

## *For students:*

Welcome to *The People's Poet Transformed*, a textbook designed to assist teachers and students with the new Transformation Task that has been introduced to the Australian English Curriculum in the senior years.

This book provides a range of poems and short stories by South Australian poet Geoff Goodfellow to use as 'springboards' for the Transformation Task. Each poem or short story is introduced by Geoff and accompanied by a set of activities to encourage you to look at various text types, devices and structures in your creative writing. There is also a chapter dedicated to how you construct a good Writer's Statement, with relevant support materials.

The poems and stories selected for this book reflect on romantic love, family relationships, domestic violence, drug and alcohol abuse, PTSD, social history and migration, class, work, health, place and community. See Geoff performing his work: check out his website and look for him on YouTube.

Geoff's writing is a wonderful springboard for the Transformation Task and I hope the ideas in this book inspire you to be creative in the texts that you produce this year!

# Poem for Annie

## Themes

Domestic Violence
The Cycle of Violence
Revenge

## Text Types

TV Advertising Campaign
Report – Psychological Assessment
Diary

Geoff Goodfellow's context statement for:

# Poem for Annie

When my sister Annie came to stay with me and my family with two teeth missing and stitches in her bottom lip, I had the opportunity to witness close-hand the effects of male violence against women. Annie stayed with us for about a month as she recovered from a beating by her partner, Brian. I began to write this poem after a week of close observation of Annie and her circumstances.

I often stay up late writing, and in the early hours of one morning I looked up to see Annie standing in front of me in the doorway. *What do you want, fang*? I asked. *How dare you speak to me like that*, she replied. *Relax, Annie.* I said, *It's times like these if you don't laugh, you'll cry, and if you start to cry, you mightn't stop.*

Annie told me she couldn't get to sleep and offered to do some of my typing. I knocked her back, telling her she should be resting and that I had to complete the work myself. After she went back to bed a piece of silver foil on the carpet near the doorway caught my eye. I unravelled it and discovered it was the wrapping from a sedative. It struck me then that the trauma Annie was experiencing went far deeper than her physical injuries.

Earlier that evening my nephew Sam, Annie's middle son, had come through my back door grinning. He'd given us a graphic description of how he'd been around to Brian's house and belted him to even the score. My sister's response was quick and sharp. She said, *Sam, you'll never beat violence with violence. Now you've stooped to his level. I didn't want that to happen. That's why I had him charged.* Sam protested, saying, *But Mum, I warned him six months ago that if he ever touched you again he'd pay for it. I had to do it, Mum.*

After listening to my sister and Sam, I wanted to write a poem to encourage all women who have been victimised to use the justice system to hold perpetrators accountable. I sensed that my sister had regained some power by taking this approach. I also wanted to write a poem that would challenge men to think about their behaviour.

## Poem for Annie

In a space of twenty years
she's had three husbands
    three names
& three children to remember
two of them

& it's only in the past
five years
    they've worked out
who they are

but she knows about work —
    she's spent a lifetime
doing it
    typing endless words
(including these)
    or using others to answer
phones
    always too busy to check
the pedigrees
of those she stayed with
    & they've all turned out
mongrels
    that couldn't/wouldn't
work

they beat her badly in each deal
    or in the middle of the night
& she looked on while friends
got diamond rings
    & learned to hide when she got
black ones

& then she met Brian
poor
poor
mis-understood Brian
who needed a mother
not a wife

but they never married
she just lived with him —
'til he jammed a glass
into her face
smashed two teeth
& slashed her lower lip

but she's laid charges now —
& that's a first

*but only because he showed*
*no remorse*
was what she told me

& when her second son informed
her that he'd found him
& smashed him in the face
with his motor-bike helmet
'til he cried *NO MORE*
she cried

*you'll never beat violence*
*with violence*

& it isn't just her hair that's
fair

*but mum*
*i warned him when he*
*blackened y' eye six months ago*
*i told him i wasn't a kid*
*to tell a lie*

her stitches came out yesterday
& make-up will hide that
slightly visible scar

the deeper one she's been working on
with sedatives

& the crowns go on
in two weeks time
so i can't call her *fang*

& i can only hope that then
she'll never be crowned
again.

## Ideas for transformation

# Poem for Annie

In this poem Annie speaks the line *you'll never beat violence with violence* and Geoff simply reports it. 'Poem for Annie' portrays the strength of victims in the most devastating circumstances. It speaks of the impact domestic violence has on women and children and the way male violence is perpetuated in our broader community. 'Poem for Annie' presents the audience with a number of different voices, which lend themselves to a range of possibilities for transformation.

## Transformation Task 1: TV Advertising Campaign

### Domestic Violence

Annie's poignant response to her son when he tried to deal with Brian on his terms was *you'll never beat violence with violence*. Despite having experienced domestic violence in previous relationships it was the first time that Annie had laid charges. Create a TV advertising campaign designed to educate the public on the ramifications of family violence. Place an emphasis on encouraging people to go to the police or other relevant agencies to get support for victims and their families. In 2016 the Australian Federal Government released an advertisement on domestic violence, which can provide you with a helpful example of a recent TV ad campaign. The ad and a range of resources can be found at **www.respect.gov.au**.

## Transformation Task 2: Report - Psychological Assessment

### The Cycle of Violence

Psychological reports are commonly used as part of the court process to determine the impact of events/situations on victims and perpetrators. In 'Poem for Annie' Geoff sarcastically describes the perpetrator as *poor/poor/mis-understood Brian.* Statistics show that perpetrators have often been victims of violence or other forms of trauma in their formative years. While domestic violence is completely unacceptable, perpetrators often have their own story that can be explored. Write a report that outlines the psychological issues that could contribute to the behaviour exhibited by perpetrators like Brian.

Alternatively the psychological report could focus on Annie or Sam and the mental and emotional impact the abuse has had on them.

## Transformation Task 3: Diary

### Revenge

Annie, like so many women, was a repeat victim of domestic violence over the years. The impact of violence affects the victim and the broader family, especially children who grow up witnessing the violence. Write a diary from Sam's perspective reflecting on his decision to turn to violence when he heard his mother had become a victim once again. The entry/entries might reflect on the trauma Sam may have experienced growing up, the sense of masculinity he held by nominating himself as his mother's protector, and his response to his mother's reaction when she was told that he'd beaten Brian in revenge.

# Don't Call Me Lad

## Themes

Family Expectations

Adolescence

Parent/Child Relationships

## Text Types

Blog

Memoir

Song Lyric

Geoff Goodfellow's context statement for:

# Don't Call Me Lad

I was thirty-eight when I wrote this poem, and had three teenage sons. At the time I was working as poet-in-residence in juvenile detention centres and prisons, as well as giving readings and conducting workshops at outer suburban high schools in low socio-economic areas. I recognised that a lot of young fellas never had a public voice. Not only that, many of them never saw language as power; they only recognised power as something physical.

One day I took my three school-age sons to meet a mate who had recently been released from prison. I introduced them as *my three lads*. My eldest, seventeen at the time, later took me to task for referring to him as a 'lad'. Not long after that I went into 'B' Division at Yatala Labour Prison one night to conduct a writing workshop. There I ran into Robert, a young bloke I knew who had recently been transferred from a youth detention centre to prison. I couldn't remember his name momentarily and greeted him with, *G'day lad*. He made me feel quite uncomfortable, and it was driven home to me then that the term *lad* can register as a real insult to the growing masculinity of young men.

'Don't Call Me Lad' touches on the way that boys want to test their physicality in relation to their fathers – and also learn where they sit in the male pecking order. I used to spar around with my old man in the sixties and wear him out quickly. After a few minutes he'd often be repeating, *Leave me alone… leave me alone*. My older sons in the eighties wanted to spar around with me and we'd often go at it for quite a while. But by the time my youngest started in the early nineties I was beginning to sound like my father.

In my work with disengaged students I've noticed that many boys seem to have given up on the idea of success or achievement through the school system. These boys often go home to a parent or parents, or caregivers, who really wouldn't have a clue about algebra or know the difference between an adjective and a verb. I remember meeting one boy who arrived late to class after attending a job interview. Knowing he'd missed out on the job, the boy commented that he would get belted that night by his old man. His dad had left school at fourteen and had worked as a council labourer all his working life. This was the mid-eighties when youth unemployment was at an all-time high. His dad was out of touch with the difficulties his own son was facing.

The tone of the poem was influenced by my surroundings. It's aggressive and rebellious, like the lives of many teenagers who are living on the edge. When I wrote it I was listening to The Smiths, The Sex Pistols, The Clash and other punk groups my sons had on the turntable at home. Our house resounded with the aggression, rebelliousness and outrageous irreverence of youth that was coming out of the UK at that time.

# Don't Call Me Lad

Don't call me lad
                    dad
just don't call me lad
got more hair on my balls dad
than y'v got
                    or had

i'm eighteen years old man
& i'll sink or i'll swim
just don't call me lad
                    dad
my name is James
                    or just Jim

& now that i vote dad
my party is green
get away with those flags dad
red & blue are both mean

y' can roll up y'r sleeves dad
& slip on y'r tie
y' can rant & lay guilt trips
but i'll spit in y'r eye

yeah i grow some plants dad
but i'm keeping it cool
four's not a plantation
i'm not such a fool

i just can't find a job dad
year twelve was a waste
two friends have just died dad
too much of a taste

yeah i get the dole dad
though it don't do much good
but don't call me lad
                                dad
i'd work if i could

now i'm mellowing out man
this home-grown is just wild
so don't call me lad
                                dad
i'm no longer a child

so don't call me lad
                                dad
i'm no longer a child.

## Ideas for transformation

# Don't Call Me Lad

The struggle of adolescence is a universal experience conveyed in 'Don't Call Me Lad'. This poem captures the voice of a teenage boy as he rails against his father's expectations and strives to find his own identity. The tone is aggressive as Geoff wants to convey the rebellion of teenage boys as they challenge the authority of their fathers. On page 108 you can Read Geoff's own transformation of this poem into 'Don't Look So Glum' with his writer's statement following.

## Transformation Task 1: Blog

### Adolescence

One of the key themes of 'Don't Call Me Lad' is growing up and the universal experience of adolescents forging an identity independent of their parents. It highlights the angst that teenagers often feel as they deal with the challenges of balancing their own needs and wants with the hopes and desires their parents may have for them. Create a blog that focuses on dealing with the challenges of adolescence from the perspective of a parent/carer. The blog could be an entry or series of entries about various aspects of raising teenagers for other parents/carers. It could also be a blog that provides helpful information for teenagers about how they manage these issues at home. Think about the tone that would best convey the information to your intended audience.

## Transformation Task 2: Memoir

### Family Expectations

Memoirs explore a personal experience as a narrative. Rather than highlighting a range of issues/challenges, a memoir can focus on a situation, anecdote or experience that has shaped the writer. Write a memoir from the point of view of a teenager about how family expectations have impacted on your life so far. It might be helpful to begin by brainstorming examples of situations where you have learnt something about yourself, about others or about the world around you. The tone of a memoir varies as it depends on the writer's experience. What tone do you want to convey in your memoir?

## Transformation Task 3: Song Lyric

### Parent/Child Relationships

'Don't Call Me Lad' is Geoff's insight into the relationship between father and teenage son. The tone of the poem is aggressive. It helps convey the tense battle between parent and child as the lines of responsibility shift. For some teenagers this may not be an accurate reflection of their experience. Are they just seeking approval from their parents? Will their choices ultimately make them happy, or their parents happy? Write a song about your experience of your relationship with your parents. Geoff referenced a range of punk bands that he listened to as he wrote this poem, which would have helped with the overall mood and tone of the text. Think about the tone you want to convey in your lyrics and the style of song that would best reflect that tone: rap, hip hop, country, ballad, pop etc. You may also want to employ the technique of rhyme as Geoff has done in his poem.

# An Uncertain Future

## Themes

Addictions

Making Choices

Judgement (Feminist Lens)

## Text Types

Feature Article

Narrative

Opinion Column

Geoff Goodfellow's context statement for:

## An Uncertain Future

'An Uncertain Future' uses the image of a woman I noticed one day as I drove through Victoria Square in Adelaide on my way to meet a mate for lunch. She caught my eye as she walked away from me across the square. She was slim and tanned and wore a denim mini skirt with strappy sandals. When I reached Gouger Street she was at the traffic lights three metres away from my car. She was standing side-on to me and I was shocked to see she was about seven months pregnant.

While we were waiting on a change of lights she raised her hand and took a drag on a cigarette. She blew out the smoke as she passed in front of my car and I noticed her teeth were blackened and broken. She was heading in the direction of the Magistrates Court and I thought with teeth like that she might be on her way to face drug-related charges. Her future and that of her unborn baby seemed so uncertain.

With my car parked I bumped into a friend who stopped to enquire about my health. This barrister was cross-examining me about my recovery from throat cancer but I couldn't provide him with definitive answers.

I walked on, thinking about the uncertainties of life – and the ways we create our own uncertainties.

The first draft of 'An Uncertain Future' was written later that afternoon.

'An Uncertain Future' was originally published in *Waltzing with Jack Dancer: a slow dance with cancer* (Wakefield Press 2011) as well as *The Best Australian Poems 2011* edited by John Tranter (Black Inc. 2011), and appeared in large-print format as a piece of public art on the courtyard wall of the Supreme Court of South Australia, as part of the Adelaide City Council and State Government arts initiative 'Splash Adelaide' during the 2012 Adelaide Festival of Arts.

## An Uncertain Future

I was sitting in my car opposite
the Adelaide Magistrates Court
    waiting on a change of lights
when i first saw her

she was in her early twenties
    had on a black sleeveless top
& a denim mini skirt
    her arms & legs were heavily
tanned & she wore strappy sandals

her hair was bottle blonde —
    & as she crossed in front of me
blowing out a stream of blue
cigarette smoke
    i noticed her black roots
complemented her chipped & broken
front teeth

she was at least seven months pregnant

the lights changed
    i moved off slowly —
into my own uncertain future.

Ideas for transformation

# An Uncertain Future

In 'An Uncertain Future' Geoff is shocked by the choices the woman is making. His account of how this poem came about reveals a number of assumptions he has made about her from his position of relative privilege (as a male). The situation may look and feel very different from the woman's point of view.

Geoff's commentary about the woman's choices is turned on himself with his final line *'i moved off slowly/into my own uncertain future'*. Sometimes observing or writing about others can lead us to examine our own choices and points of view. Writing from a perspective other than your own requires imagination and empathy.

## Transformation Task 1: Feature Article

### Addictions

In 'An Uncertain Future' the woman is smoking. It is also suggested that she may be a drug user. Along with alcoholism, these are relatively common addictions. People can also be addicted to things such as gambling, eating, shopping, gaming or sex. Substance abuse can threaten relationships, health, employment and general security in life. Write a feature article that deals with the impact of addictions on individuals, their families, friends and the broader community. Contact local or government organisations that deal with addictions and conduct research such as interviews to ensure your article is authentic.

## Transformation Task 2: Narrative

### Making Choices

'An Uncertain Future' highlights how the choices we make can affect others and either broaden or limit our own opportunities. Initially the poem is about the choices of the young woman Geoff sees but then the perspective shifts back to his own life with his final line *into my own uncertain future*. Write a short narrative with the central theme exploring the idea of making choices titled 'An Uncertain Future'.

## Transformation Task 3: Opinion Column

### Judgement (Feminist Lens)

This poem is based on Geoff's observations of an unknown woman as he drives through the city of Adelaide. A number of assumptions are made about the woman and her circumstances, and judgements are passed about her choices as a pregnant woman, based on what he sees from his car. We know that women continue to struggle for autonomy regarding their own bodies in relation to sexual health and reproduction. Women are regularly judged by their looks; particularly what women wear as a justification for how they are treated. Write an opinion column about the issue of women being judged by their appearance, using the experience outlined in 'An Uncertain Future' as a springboard. This task could also be connected with work on Critical Theory, looking at a text through the Feminist Lens.

# Crowd Control

## Themes

Alcohol-fuelled Violence

Complexities of the Human Character

Abuse of Power

## Text Types

Editorial

Poem

Newspaper Article

Geoff Goodfellow's context statement for:

# Crowd Control

I first met Terry when he was sixteen and I was in my early twenties. A couple of years later I became his first boxing manager. Later, Terry became a champion main event fighter. In 1982 Terry knocked out Rocky St Clair at the South Sydney Leagues Club. Rocky was hospitalised and had to be put into an induced coma. He didn't leave hospital for some time and when he did, it was in a wheelchair. As much as Terry was a hard man, he was greatly affected by the damage he did to Rocky. Photographs on the front pages of newspapers of the day showed him at Rocky's bedside, tears running down his face. He was ridiculed by many in the boxing fraternity for the emotion he displayed, and soon after this Terry hung up his gloves.

Terry only completed the middle years of high school and always relied on his physicality to make an income. Without boxing, his career aspirations were limited and he began work as a bouncer at one of Adelaide's biggest suburban hotels. He had a fearsome reputation; he often left people with broken noses, teeth or ribs, if not unconscious. I worked alongside him on some occasions and often covered for Terry on nights when he couldn't work. It was on one of those nights that the inspiration for 'Crowd Control' came to me. As I was working my way through the front bar people were saying they were glad I was on tonight instead of that 'lunatic', not that any of them would have dared call Terry a lunatic to his face.

One of the patrons had his feet resting up on a chair. When I asked him to put them back on the ground he questioned who I was to give orders. I told him I was the bouncer. *No you're not'* he said, *Terry's the bouncer.* I explained that I was filling in for Terry that night. *Get your feet down,* I repeated. *And what if I don't?* he said. *I'll do it for you'* I told him. *He done this to me,* he said, pointing to his indented cheek where the bone had been compressed. I said, *Get your feet down or I'll give you a matching pair.* He brought them down then, saying, *He just would have belted me.*

'Crowd Control' is a character poem. Character poems require the writer to observe what the character *is* like, not simply what they *look* like. The way Terry used his body and his mouth to intimidate people became key elements in this poem, allowing me to bring his character to life. I also wanted to highlight the complexity of Terry's character. The image of him crying at Rocky's bedside is in direct contrast to the lack of emotion that many people witnessed as he went about his work as a bouncer.

I wrote the poem about Terry, but also for Terry, to confront him about the way he approached people and his use of violence in the way that he worked.

# Crowd Control

Terry's the bouncer
    six foot & thirteen stone

& if you're superstitious
    you could get real unlucky
with this one

he looks a cross between
a Boxer
    & a Staffordshire

& can start a blue
in an empty house (although
he'd never admit it)

in this pub
    HIS PUB
the owner
    barmen
    barmaids
    cook
& customers
    eat shit    Terry's
    & there's some big
logs amongst 'em
    'cos Terry
who used to box main events
on the east coast as
    The Blonde Bomber

is crowd control

he's known by his
train track knuckles
    steel blue eyes
    flat filleted nose
    & when his slow
deliberate drawl drones
down the bar
    *don't get y'r aspirations*
*mixed up with y'r abilities*
*MUG don't*

but if you reckon you've
got form he'll ask
    *are you insured —*
*get out here on the lawn*
*where y' won't hit y'r head*
*on the way down STUPID*

now i'm not religious
    but if you go —
may the good Lord
    or three of your best mates
be with you

the customer with the
compressed cheek bone
calls him *Sir* now
    the police *Mister*
others out of earshot
    call him a lunatic
others out of hours
    call him on the phone
where they can't be reached

he deals out punishment
like a croupier
    he's not scared by
        aces
            jokers
                clubs
                    or jacks

but he's got a soft spot

found it one night in a Leagues
Club in Sydney
    knocked a bloke into a coma
in 'The Eighth'

cried for 3 days —

*soft* they said
    *bit bloody soft*
*oughta give the game away*

& he did
    except in this pub.

## Ideas for transformation

# Crowd Control

Among other things, 'Crowd Control' is a commentary on pub and club violence. It highlights the potential dangers of being part of a drinking culture, not only from other patrons but also at the hands of those being paid to keep you safe. Written in 1984, 'Crowd Control' shows that alcohol-fuelled violence is nothing new. It is most disturbingly manifested today in the phenomenon of the 'coward's punch', which has become a national issue for young males.

A feature of this poem is the use of puns and double entendre to create layers of meaning. The tasks below provide opportunities to play with words and word meanings to engage the audience.

## Transformation Task 1: Editorial

### Alcohol-fuelled Violence

'Crowd Control' highlights the issue of violence in places where alcohol is served and consumed. Alcohol-fuelled violence is not new, but in recent years we have seen the rise of the phenomenon of the 'coward's punch', unprovoked violent attacks that have left a number of young men dead. Some would argue that alcohol is not the cause of increasingly violent behaviour but that violence is symptomatic of society failing to deal with broader issues. In recent years a range of laws and policies have been put in place to attempt to make pub and club culture safer. Write an editorial that discusses the issues associated with Australia's drinking culture titled 'Alcohol-fuelled Violence is a Myth'.

## Transformation Task 2: Poem

### Complexities of the Human Character

'Crowd Control' is a character poem. On the one hand Terry appears merciless in his work as a bouncer but he is also deeply affected by the suffering he has inflicted on another person. Write an original character poem about someone you have observed. It might be a person in your family, a friend, a teacher or someone in the local neighbourhood. A character poem creates a vivid portrait of a person. It shows not just what they look like, but how they behave, how they speak, their mannerisms, attitudes and opinions. It should capture the complexities of their character.

## Transformation Task 3: Newspaper Article

### Abuse of Power

Terry uses his position of power in the pub to abuse and intimidate people. Write a newspaper article reporting on a situation where a person has abused their position of power. It might be a bouncer who has used excessive force against a patron, a school administering unfair consequences, a police officer abusing his/her position, or a company exploiting its workers. You may choose to use current events locally or globally as inspiration for your article.

# Reminders

## Themes

Romantic Love

Grief and Loss

Life Choices

## Text Types

Letter

Eulogy

Movie Poster/Trailer

Geoff Goodfellow's context statement for:

# Reminders

I'm known for using language that is harsh and direct but for this poem I knew a more gentle approach was required. 'Reminders' tenderly records the sense of loss I felt at the end of a relationship. It's about the way we continue to carry people in our minds, if not in our hearts, long after they have gone.

'Reminders' was written six days after the ending of my relationship with a contemporary dancer in the early nineties. She was offered a once-in-a-lifetime opportunity to audition for the Batsheva Dance Company in Israel. We decided to end our relationship so she could pursue her career overseas and a week later she packed her bags and left.

A few nights after she'd gone I noticed a strand of long brown hair lying on my bedspread. With care I picked it up and held it between my thumb and forefinger. I began talking to this hair as if it were my lover, still feeling her presence even though she had left. I placed it on my dressing table and as I did, I noticed the tube of lipgloss she had left behind on my dresser. Moments later, lying in bed, my nostrils filled with her scent from deep within my pillow. With these reminders, I knew there was a poem to be written.

Some hours later, after six drafts, I had written 'Reminders'.

## Reminders

You left several strands
of hair
    scattered across my
sheets

you left your yellow
toothbrush
    on the top shelf
of my bathroom cabinet

you left your white lacy
G-string
    in the pocket of my
bathrobe

you left your pink lipgloss
with the glitter
    on my dressing table

you left my alarm clock
    set at 6:45 am

you left your new novel
by Gabriel Garcia Marquez
    unread

we both left so much
    unsaid

but most of all
    you left your scent
buried deep inside my
pillow
    & even though it's been
six nights now and i've changed

the bed linen
    rearranged the bathroom
cabinet & the dressing table —
placed your book in my bookcase
    thrown out your G-string
    your lipgloss
& your yellow toothbrush

your scent is making my eyes
watery
    & still    i can't escape you.

Ideas for transformation

# Reminders

'Reminders' focuses on the sense of loss at the end of a significant relationship. It can be a hard thing for a person to accept the end of a relationship when there has been no particular conflict that brings about its demise. Letting go of a loved one can be traumatic. The poem makes us think about difficult choices we can be faced with regarding the kind of life we want for ourselves and for those we care about. While concrete reminders of people may be discarded, we can carry on meaningful interactions with people in our minds and hearts long after they have gone. Love in its various forms is a universal human experience and the subject of some of our most influential and timeless literature. Exploring our most important relationships and how they make us feel provides endless opportunities for our writing.

## Transformation Task 1: Letter

### Romantic Love

Geoff writes candidly about missing someone he cared about deeply. Write a letter from the perspective of the dancer about her decision to leave and pursue a new life in a new country. Explore how she feels about the end of the relationship; maybe she is grieving too or perhaps she has moved on. What might her 'reminders' be?

## Transformation Task 2: Eulogy

### Grief and Loss

Sometimes we choose to move away from people who are significant in our life. At other times we are separated by circumstances beyond our control such as death. In either circumstance we experience grief and loss, both of the person and of our dreams and expectations. Write a eulogy for someone significant focusing on the things you will remember about them most and the impact they had on your life. Alternatively, you could write your own eulogy featuring aspects of your life that you would wish to be remembered for.

## Transformation Task 3: Movie Poster/Trailer

### Life Choices

Sometimes we face situations where we have to make difficult, potentially life-altering decisions. These choices can have an impact on important relationships, opportunities, and our overall happiness. Do we follow a new career path? Do we move to a new city? Do we begin a new relationship? Geoff's poem 'Reminders' is as much about the important decisions we might be faced with in life as it is about romantic love. Design a movie trailer on the theme of making difficult life choices.

# Maybe

## Themes

Anti-Smoking
The Power of Advertising
Multinational Corporations

## Text Types

Print Advertisement
Exposition
Journal Article

Geoff Goodfellow's context statement for:

# Maybe

I was diagnosed with throat cancer in 2008. My surgeon commented that I was young to be having a neck dissection. I was fifty-seven years of age. When I woke from surgery in the Head and Neck ward at the Royal Adelaide Hospital, I was surrounded by five other men who were all at least ten years older. We all had working class backgrounds and had been 'hands and feet' workers and heavy smokers. Brands of cigarettes were discussed among us one morning, as were the number of cigarettes smoked each day.

At the height of his career Paul Hogan was one of Australia's most beloved actors and comedians and became known as the quintessential Aussie larrikin after his title role in the 1984 film *Crocodile Dundee*. In the seventies he was the face of the Winfield cigarette brand in an extremely successful TV advertising campaign that targeted working class people. The ad showed Paul Hogan in a dinner suit and bow tie, hair neatly combed, flicking open a pack of Winfield and saying, *Anyhow, have a Winfield* in a broad Australian accent. This became a catch phrase among working class Australian men, who are known for their love of mimicry.

I enjoy wordplay and have used puns on popular tobacco brands throughout the poem.

Cigarette advertising on TV and radio ceased in 1976 but prevailed in print until 1989. As I looked around the ward it was abundantly clear how effective, and how damaging, these campaigns had been. Paul Hogan, the beloved Aussie icon who'd made me laugh as a teenager, certainly wasn't making me laugh now. In the end, the joke is on the smoker.

'Maybe' highlights the power of the media and the need for it to be held accountable for the messages it delivers. The image of the stapled throat provides a stark warning to would-be smokers. I wrote the poem to deliver a strong anti-smoking message and critique the large corporations that profit from people's misfortune.

## Maybe

In the Head & Neck ward
most of us blokes are fifty plus
    old Marlboro men
on Alpine white beds
    now that's Kool

& i'll give you the Drum
    it could well be Winfield
Reds on the right
    & Blues on the left
(geez    that looks like Blue
in bed seven
    hasn't he lost some weight)
& where is Paul Hogan
when we really need a laugh

post op now with stapled
throats after our neck dissections

maybe it'll hurt too much

maybe there's nothing much
to laugh at anymore

maybe now    the laugh's
    on us.

## Ideas for transformation

# Maybe

In Australia, ongoing legislation to minimise the advertising, sale and consumption of cigarettes in shared public spaces has resulted in a dramatic shift away from smoking in the community, especially among teenagers. The poem 'Maybe' describes the dangers of tobacco and the impact advertising had on an unsuspecting public in a time when smoking was commonplace. While the large multinational companies of the tobacco industry raked in huge profits on the back of clever advertising and celebrity endorsements, the risks associated with smoking were withheld from the general public for decades. This is just one example of the influence of the media in our society.

## Transformation Task 1: Print Advertisement

### Anti-Smoking

The poem 'Maybe' recounts Geoff's very personal experience with the adverse effects of smoking. He is a strong anti-smoking campaigner and uses his story to drive home the terrible impact smoking can have on your health. This poem is a great springboard for an anti-smoking campaign. Design a print advertisement using the poem 'Maybe' and Geoff's personal story to educate about the dangers of smoking.

## Transformation Task 2: Exposition

### The Power of Advertising

The poem 'Maybe' identifies the powerful impact that celebrities can have on the public when it comes to advertising products and services. Paul Hogan, the much-loved comedian, ultimately becomes synonymous with Geoff's cancer diagnosis. Write an exposition on the topic 'Celebrities should be held accountable for the impact of the products they advertise.'

## Transformation Task 3: Journal Article

### Multinational Corporations

Geoff has cleverly used puns throughout 'Maybe', highlighting popular cigarette brands and the way they were marketed to an unsuspecting public, particularly working class people. Cigarette advertising was so successful that some brands were linked to the world's largest multinational companies. Over time it became apparent that the tobacco industry was aware of the dangers of their products and deliberately misled the public about the risks. Write a journal article on the topic 'Multinational corporations are only interested in their profit margins.' The article could focus on the tobacco industry or another area of interest. To assist your article read about Jeffrey Wigand, a whistle blower in the tobacco industry, whose story was the basis of the film *The Insider* (1999) directed by Michael Mann.

# The Colour Blue

## Themes

Family

Alcoholism

The Power of Language

## Text Types

Autobiography

Review

Poem/Narrative

Geoff Goodfellow's context statement for:

## The Colour Blue

One Sunday morning I was putting together the manuscript for *Poems for a Dead Father*. The publisher had asked for a photo of my dad for the front cover and one of me for the back. As I pulled photos from a box and spread them over the kitchen table I noticed that in every image I found of my dad, he was drunk. It had often been painful to see him that way, but sometimes it had been quite amusing. Now here he was, nearly five years after his death, drunk at my kitchen table. I was laughing out loud, imagining him trying to navigate the back steps then bumping off the walls of my hallway and into the kitchen.

Despite my dad's alcoholism I always felt connected to him and it is the strength and colour of his eyes that remain my strongest memory. That morning I realised I was looking for a photo of him that didn't really exist. His blue eyes were closed or averted in each and every image. Apart from his black and white WWII enlistment photo hanging in my hallway, in almost every other photo I had of him there was a drink in one hand, a smoke in the other. The title 'The Colour Blue' refers to the strength of his gaze, which commanded your attention, yet always remained comforting.

### View Geoff's photographs

The four photos featured in the poem can be viewed online:

**www.geoffgoodfellow.com**

Click on Study Guide for ***Poems for a Dead Father***

## The Colour Blue

You've been dead for nearly
five years now dad
    you never got to climb
the three concrete steps
to my back door in Nelson Street
(that would've been a challenge)
    you never got to bounce
off the walls of the hallway
before finding the kitchen either
    so i was a bit surprised
to find you last Sunday
    drunk at my kitchen table

you were spread over it

i'd pulled out a box of photos
looking for myself
when i found you
    you said nothing of course —
but you still made me laugh
    understatement or gesture —
i'm buggered if i know

but you were there
    alone & drunk at my kitchen
table    your eyes closed
    your tie loosened —
& your nicotined fingers
holding the cigarette you were
dragging on

& then you were there again
    with mum this time —
& Mark nestled in-between
nursing a beer & looking
surprisingly sober
    again with your eyes closed
& your mouth wide open
    empty bottles & half-full
glasses surround you
    a bottle of tomato sauce
sits on a table in the foreground
    it must have been a barbie

& again
    with mum & Anne this time—
& though they are both smiling
for the camera
    (mum somewhat nervously —
& Anne looking as innocent as
an ageing Shirley Temple)
    you're slumped in a green
kitchen chair wearing a grey suit
    your grey hair slicked down
& the part to the right is true
    your chin rests on your chest
& your eyes lead to the floor
    a cigarette burns
in an outstretched hand
    the beer on the floor looks
empty
    you could easily be muttering
*get a cab    we're goin' home*

& then i've found you with my mate
Melbourne Jack
    & he was looking good —

fresh out of 'B' Division
at Yatala
    he'd just done seven straight
& you were at his side
going *wah wah wah*
    Jack was smiling
but turning away from you
    trying to disengage

i remember that afternoon

Jack came over after i snapped
that shot & said
    *listen Geoff i've never called*
*the coppers on anyone but if your*
*old man doesn't get out of my ear*
    *i'll ring the jacks & get him*
*pinched for assaulting ear drums*

Jack can't ring anyone now
    he's gone too but that's life —
or death

looking at those photos now
    i can still hear your nasal
tone
    & even though your eyes are
closed or averted in each & every
frame
    i can still see the colour
blue
    can still remember the strength
of your gaze
    can still remember how clearly
your eyes spoke.

Ideas for transformation

## The Colour Blue

'The Colour Blue' gives us an experience of Geoff's father through a series of family photos. The voices and stories of other people in the photos are also brought to life. The title of the poem is the recurring motif, referencing the colour of Geoff's father's eyes, which is the strongest memory he has of him. The title 'The Colour Blue' also hints at the mood of the poem. Images can be powerful and stay with us - even though they are only a snapshot of a moment in time. Geoff's poem is a wonderful example of how the use of language can reveal considerably more about the thoughts and feelings of the people photographed.

### Transformation Task 1: Autobiography

#### Family

This poem is centred on Geoff's experience of his father, how he remembers him and the impact he had on his life. Write an autobiographical account of an experience with a family member that has shaped your life. The event or situation may seem relatively insignificant yet uncover an important message about the relationship you have with that person.

## Transformation Task 2: Review

### Alcoholism

Geoff's poem about his father reveals that he suffered from alcoholism. Although there were many times when his dad's drinking caused great concern for the family, in this poem Geoff remembers him with humour and tenderness. The impact of alcoholism varies for each family and is extremely complex. Write a review that tackles the issue of alcoholism or living with a family member who suffers from an addiction. Include a range of perspectives and possible recommendations.

## Transformation Task 3: Poem/Narrative

### The Power of Language

'The Colour Blue' was conceived by Geoff while sorting through old family photos and reminiscing about his dad. Choose a photo or series of photos of someone or something significant in your life. In the same way Geoff wrote about his father using the four photos on his kitchen table, write a poem or narrative using language to bring out things a photo can't necessarily capture, such as smells, sounds, associations and thoughts.

# Semaphore

## Themes

Cultural Diversity
Social Inequality (Marxist Lens)
The Importance of Place

## Text Types

Feature Article
Opinion Column
Poem

Geoff Goodfellow's context statement for:

# Semaphore

This is a love poem to my suburb.

Despite living most of my adult life in Semaphore, I'd never written about it until the publication of *Semi Madness: voices from Semaphore* in 1997. Semaphore is an interesting place with an eclectic community where you can be who you want to be.

Many successful sports people live in Semaphore, especially footballers because it's a stone's throw from AAMI Stadium and Alberton Oval. In the nineties you'd often see a gold Rolls Royce parked alongside a beat-up Morris Minor on Semaphore Road. These days you'll find AFL players sipping lattes at outside cafe tables while nearby you'll be stopped and asked for spare change by one of the many characters who live in the various hostels supporting people with mental health issues or addictions.

At one time I lived in South Terrace, a wide, tree-lined street with homes in the million dollar bracket. A few streets away there were fibro houses where people lived difficult lives. These contrasts prompted me to write a collection of poems to record my suburb and its people.

By the mid-nineties I was living upstairs in the Federal Hotel and spending a lot of time at the sidewalk cafes on Semaphore Road. I came to know many of the people living in hostels and would often drink coffee with them during the day. As much as I'm a good talker, I'm a good listener too, and I enjoyed hearing their stories, snippets of which you'll hear throughout the poem.

I was sitting at a coffee shop on Semaphore Road one day contemplating the archangel that looks down from the war memorial on the foreshore. I wondered what some of the hostel residents thought about it, knowing that people with mental health issues sometimes gravitate towards religion. Then I shifted my gaze to the flag flying out the front of the RSL club and considered the freedoms that have been fought for in our society. It seemed to me that so many people in Semaphore are still fighting for freedom in their everyday lives – including some who frequent the RSL.

This poem is a commentary on the inequalities that exist in our society from one side of the street to the other. It calls on the Semaphore community to celebrate and be proud while striving to take better care of itself.

## Semaphore

Semaphore
    you are so full of bad taste —
you've half convinced me
you're good taste

but i love you Semaphore

you have a main street
that wanders down to the sea
like a good old fashioned
country town
    maybe you are a country town
Semaphore
    lost on the outskirts
of a city

but Semaphore
    don't be embarrassed —
you are the only suburb in this
city where people can still
shop in their pyjamas without
being gigged

Semaphore
    you are so unpretentious —
so up-front honest
    that at times you delight me

Semaphore
    you are all larrikins
& character
    if you're not a manic depressive
or a schizophrenic
    if you're not a liberal

a labor a pinko or a greenie
    if you're not a separatist
feminist lesbian
    a lipstick lesbian
or a builders' labourer
    if you're not a Rolls Royce driver
or a Kingswood owner
    if you're not a Catholic
an Anglican a Pentecostal or an
agnostic
    if you're not a renter nor an
owner
    if you're not a yuppie
a trendoid
a straight
a gay
a trannie
a drunk
an addict
or a dead-beat
    if you don't have a ring
on your finger —
or through your nose
your eyebrow
your nipple
or your foreskin
    if you don't dig hip hop
be bop   blues   acid jazz   funk
rockabilly   rap   techno   jungle
ska   reggae   pop   house
or classical
    chances are —
Semaphore
    is not yet ready for you

Semaphore
    you are so laid back i'm sure
there are days when everyone is so
relaxed
    that no one in the suburb
wakes up

Semaphore
    you confuse me each summer
by inviting me in for a swim
    but then you make me walk a mile
just to get my thighs wet
    you're a tease Semaphore

but you tease others too

you let your jetty shrink
each winter
    & by summer —
when half of South Australia
have stubbed a toe on a boardwalk
    no one wants to say they own it

you tease & you shame

you've teased so many of your
old age pensioners
by putting pokie machines
on Semaphore Road

but you have shamed yourself too
Semaphore

you have denied so many of your
invalid pensioners
a sporting chance at a whiz bang
centre

or is walking down Semaphore Road
with your hand out considered to be
cultural tourism?
maybe Semaphore —
you need to direct that question
to the Liberal government

but why do these invalid pensioners
ask for anything Semaphore?

maybe fish patties & mashed potatoes
stale cakes & stale bread
cold showers & no soap
cold rooms in winter
& hot boxes in summer
365 days a year are boring —
(nothing too liberal about that lot)

Semaphore
i came to you in the 60s when
your pubs were full of wharfies
& your road was frantic

now the wharves are used for little
more than fishing
your front bars are as empty
as your churches
& your road is frantic
for other reasons

i saunter now & enjoy & savour you
Semaphore
i've got time to stop on your
otherwise bland footpath & talk to
Bobby & listen to his repetitive
chatter

  i've got time to stop outside of
'Larrikins' & dance with Dorothy
while she sings
'Tiptoe Through the Tulips'
  i've got time to stop outside
'Flour Power Bakery' & say
*good morning gentleman* to Wally
  & hear him reply
*good morning sir & good morning*
*to you too young lady* to my
four-year-old
  & i've got time for Gerald —
posted once again outside the 'Federal'
& smacking his lips while waiting
waiting waiting for enough to buy
another can
  & sure enough   as if on cue —
as we draw near he'll call out to my
daughter
  *that's a lovely hat you are wearing*
*today my dear   you're a very good girl*
*aren't you*
  & i've got time to stop & let
Bob Lumley kiss me on the cheek
if he needs to
  that is   if he hasn't got
Tom the greengrocer already —
& that's about the end of the option
plan for Bob
  & i've got time to look up & see
the flag flying from the mast of
the RSL club
  & be challenged to consider
what other freedoms

we are still fighting for
    & i've got time too —
to look up at the archangel watching
over Semaphore Road from the Esplanade
    & i contemplate the comfort
she might give to some
with her outstretched wings
    & i've had time strolling down
Semaphore Road toward the Esplanade
    to recognise that the Chinese Maple
trees that sit in pairs
all along the median strip
    are weaker by the time they hit
the coast
    by the time they hit the edge —
by the time they have
    no other place to go.

## Ideas for transformation

# Semaphore

Semaphore is an important place to Geoff. This poem expresses Geoff's love for the suburb that has seen him through many life experiences and milestones over the years. Place can shape who we are and what is important to us, reinforcing our values in the same way experiences and people can. Exploring the significance of place is integral to many texts. 'Semaphore' is also a commentary on the inequalities that exist in our society.

## Transformation Task 1: Feature Article

### Cultural Diversity

Imagine you are a local news reporter for the Semaphore area. Using information from Geoff's poem write a feature article that celebrates the cultural diversity of Semaphore. This could form part of a tourism campaign to bring people to the area. Similarly, you could write a feature article about your own suburb.

## Transformation Task 2: Opinion Column

### Social Inequality (Marxist Lens)

In 'Semaphore' Geoff highlights the many contrasts between the people who make this suburb their home, in particular, the stark difference between the 'haves' and 'have nots'. While Geoff conveys a unique sense of cohesion and genuine acceptance of all kinds of people, things might look very different from the point of view of the marginalised. Write an opinion column that outlines the social inequality expressed in the poem. You may choose to investigate life from the point of view of one of the groups identified in the poem, presenting an alternative perspective on the inequality in Semaphore. This task could also be connected to work done in Critical Theory, looking at a text through a Marxist Lens.

## Transformation Task 3: Poem

### The Importance of Place

Geoff had lived in Semaphore for many years before he wrote about the place he has called home for the majority of his adult life. The poem 'Semaphore' encapsulates the strong personal connection he has with his suburb. Geoff uses the device of personification, 'talking' to Semaphore as if it were his lover or an old friend. Place can have a powerful way of impressing itself on our memory. Using personification write a poem that draws upon your experience of a significant place. It may be a place where you find peace or solitude such as a beach, park, city or distant home. It may also be a place of significance to you because important memories were created there.

# Miles Away & A Mirror to My Childhood

## Themes

War/Conflict

Mental Illness - PTSD (Psychoanalytical Lens)

The Impact of War on Families

## Text Types

Cartoon

Letter to the Editor

Narrative

Geoff Goodfellow's context statement for:

## Miles Away & A Mirror to My Childhood

I grew up in a street full of War Service homes with a father who suffered Post Traumatic Stress Disorder (PTSD). Other close relatives and most of the men from my street had it too. The dangers faced by people who went to war and their families were therefore brought home to me on a daily basis.

As a young teenager I heard about the war in Vietnam but I had no idea where that country even was. (Working class people in the sixties generally finished school at fifteen and went to work – not travelling, like many young people do today.) Eventually I did get called up but it was my dad who helped me avoid national service and the possibility of going to war. My two poems 'Miles Away' and 'A Mirror to My Childhood' are about my experience of growing up as a child in a family affected by PTSD.

I vividly recall waking up in the early hours as a young child to my dad screaming, *Get in the trenches, get in the trenches*. And then it would be Harry screaming. He was an old army mate of my dad's who would sometimes sleep on a camp stretcher in our lounge room when he got kicked out by his wife because of his madness. I was copping their screams in stereo.

Often on a Saturday or Sunday Mum would take us four kids on two buses to visit my dad in Ward 17 at the Repatriation General Hospital (my old man referred to it as *The Nutcracker's Suite*) where many other men were suffering similarly. As I got older and started roaming beyond my own neighbourhood I discovered people living quite differently. Their streets were in sharp contrast to the streets of War Service Group Scheme houses with their surrounding semi-detached Housing Trust homes which I knew so well. Here were individually designed homes, manicured lawns, flashy cars and clothes. I was used to a dirt street with men who staggered home after six pm when the pubs closed. It didn't take much for me to realise the difference between my existence and that of the boys who lived on the other side of Regency Road: most of their fathers had avoided going to war.

Living through my father's outbursts and episodes from a young age meant that I was never under the illusion that going to war was a 'boy's own adventure'. I could also see how the men and women who did serve were failed miserably by the system when they came home. Housing and pensions don't address the lifelong mental health issues that many veterans suffer or the generational impact on families in the years that follow. My poems ‘Miles Away’ and ‘A Mirror to My Childhood’ both focus on these issues.

PTSD remains a major concern for servicemen and women returning from Iraq and Afghanistan and increasingly is becoming part of the national conversation.

## Miles Away

I remember my feet
on the cold kitchen lino
that morning
    a teenager with
bumfluff & pimples
    i was leaning over
the kitchen table
    most of its red & white
marbled laminex top
covered in the morning
newspaper

as i stood above it all
    i read there was a war
in the jungles of Vietnam
    & they were sending Aussies

Vietnam i thought
    Vietnam . . .
where the hell is Vietnam

& i found *The Jacaranda Atlas*
from school
    Vietnam    i kept thinking —
it must be next to Queensland
    but it wasn't

it took a while but i did
find it
    it was on page 75 —
& it was miles away

as i stared at the map
    i thought about the madness
the old man lived with
    & how he served
in the Middle East

& i thought about the madness
uncle Bronte lived with
    & how he served
in New Guinea

& i thought about the madness
cousin Neville lived with
    & how he served
in Korea

Vietnam    i thought
    Vietnam . . .
& i knew then
    knew then i was going —
nowhere.

# A Mirror to My Childhood

I was somewhere around forty
when i first watched that
famous Bill Bennett docudrama
*A Street to Die*
    the story of the first
Australian Vietnam vet to
challenge the government for
compo over Agent Orange

the opening scenes show a street
full of War Service Group Scheme
houses set back in the 70s
    & up there in black & white
on that little screen
    the violence
    the rage
    the drunkenness
    the terror
    the hopelessness

it was a mirror to my childhood

& throughout my little life
i had thought it only happened
in my house
    only happened in my street —
only happened with my father's
war

i thought it was a 50s thing

it was then i became aware
that it was perhaps each & every
war

 & i wondered about my
paternal grandfather . . .
 & exactly what he brought
home from France

throughout my childhood we often
had shards of glass swept across
the kitchen lino
 the old man drunk again
& opening up the louvred windows
to run his clenched fist down
& take out eight panes at a time
 it became an artform
& he'd seldom cut himself
 he had it down pat

& then it was the kitchen table
& he'd clear it
 picking up the bottle of tomato
sauce & hurling it like
a hand grenade into the duck-egg
blue wall
 it was then he'd flip
the laminex topped table
 then move along & upend
the cutlery drawer & wipe out
a few shelves of glassware
& crockery

*now clean this fuckin' mess up*
he'd scream
 & stagger off to bed —
to burn another hole in another
sheet or another pillowcase
with another Philip Morris
Executive untipped

    punching another hole through
the bedroom door to make sure
we could hear him rant & rave
    at least until the two Mogadons
that mum crushed up between two
teaspoons & slipped into
a cup of tea took hold
    but sometimes he'd go until dawn

years later we laughed about it
    suggesting that maybe he thought
he was a cartographer
    making those big red maps of
Australia in that suburban war zone

he was always remorseful the next
morning
(ever the good salesman)
    & most of the mess would have been
cleaned up by mum
    & we all forgave him
        & we forgave him
            & forgave him

& he'd go off in the morning
    dressed to kill in a suit & tie
& snap brim hat
    promising of course —
not to drink that day
    then meeting up with Big Dick Woore
& buckling for a heartstarter
    the pair of them gone AWOL
again
    propping at an inner city pub
for the day

telling yarns & spinning stories
(& often pennies)
lobbing home on the drunks' bus
or in a smash'n'grab
often without a zack to his
name
his hat & his briefcase
or one or the other missing again
waiting for him behind the bar
at *The Cri* or *The Ambassadors* or
*The Union*
or wherever else he may have
finished up

some nights though he'd lumber in
bouncing off one wall and onto
another
wanting to kiss us all . . .
& telling us he loved each & every
one of us
& confused   we'd shove him
aside
hating him   yet loving him

i remember nights i'd tie him up
with his business ties
i'd wrestle him to his
bedroom —
pin him to the bed & hog-tie him
bind his ankles & his wrists
behind his back
& then i'd gag him

that shut him up

i was nearly as big as him then
    i was probably twelve

he quietened down over the years
though
    often sober for days at a time —
& we all learned to enjoy
one another then
    there was no malice    none

he paid me back big-time when
i turned eighteen
    my number came up in the
National Service Lottery
    *don't go* he said
*i don't want you finishing up*
*as stupid as your father*
    & we read the fine print
& he saw that married persons
were exempt

Neville drove the wedding car
    i became a child groom.

Ideas for transformation

## Miles Away & A Mirror to My Childhood

These poems deal with war and the impact of PTSD on veterans and their families after WWII. Statistics show that today rates of mental illness and suicide among returning service personnel are increasing. Over the last decade the national spotlight has been directed on the way people have been supported or have lacked the necessary support to re-establish their lives successfully. Sadly, it seems it is an issue that is yet to be resolved. Meanwhile Australian troops continue to be deployed overseas.

### Transformation Task 1: Cartoon

War/Conflict

Cartoons are often used as a device for social and political commentary. In times of war they can draw attention to both perpetrators and victims. The purpose of a cartoon is to elicit a response from readers/viewers, inviting them to think about an issue and draw their own conclusions. The attacks on Charlie Hebdo speak strongly of their power. Design a war cartoon based on Geoff's experiences or more recent conflicts around the globe.

## Transformation Task 2: Letter to the Editor

### Mental Illness (Psychoanalytical Lens) PTSD

'Miles Away' and 'Mirror to My Childhood' delve into Geoff's firsthand experience of living with a returned soldier and the effects of Post Traumatic Stress Disorder (PTSD). On the news and social media there is a growing awareness of the issue of PTSD for men and women who have seen active duty. Write a letter to the editor of a newspaper outlining your concerns about PTSD and the increasing rate of suicide among returned servicemen and women. As part of your response suggest how the issue should be addressed and who is responsible for supporting these service personnel. This task could also be connected to work done on Critical Theory, looking at a text through the Psychoanalytical Lens.

## Transformation Task 3: Narrative

### The Impact of War on Families

The poems 'Miles Away' and 'Mirror to My Childhood' describe the impact of war on Geoff and his family. Imagine you are being conscripted. Using information from both poems write a short narrative about the impact on you and your family.

# The Seventh Doctor

## Themes

Challenging Authority
Humour in Adversity
The Rights of People

## Text Types

Radio Script
Monologue
Webpage

Geoff Goodfellow's context statement for:

## The Seventh Doctor

This poem critiques our Australian health care system, which sometimes seems to lose sight of the person being treated. As a public patient I was able to access life-saving services at no cost. Ultimately the system worked for me – but only because I had the ability and tenacity to self-advocate repeatedly over many months in the face of humiliation, condescension and class prejudice. I'm eternally grateful to Guy Rees, 'The Seventh Doctor', who took control of my treatment after I told him about the difficulties I was having with some of his colleagues. He even ensured I was given a personal apology by The Fifth Doctor, who had delivered my cancer diagnosis without a hint of empathy.

As I was in theatre being prepared for a major neck dissection, Dr Rees took time to encourage me to write about the difficult experiences I'd had with various health professionals. He said he'd told Robert Hannaford to paint as part of his recovery and thought it important that I should write as a part of mine. He knew my work and its themes of chronicling working class lives and examining issues of injustice. He told me too, that doctors don't often get critiqued.

One morning at my bedside I was told by The Eighth Doctor that Dr Rees had brought several of my books into the operating theatre and distributed them among the medical staff to be read aloud as I went under. That meant a lot to me. It made me aware that I was being viewed as a whole person with agency and some intelligence, rather than the inanimate object I'd been made to feel by The Fifth Doctor. I believe that had I not challenged the doctors and the treatment I received initially, I would have died.

## The Seventh Doctor

The first doctor i saw was my
local GP
    he said i had the flu
& the lump in my neck
was bunched up muscle
    he told me to go home —
drink plenty of water
& eat Panadeine Forte & Valium

i saw him again five days later
& told him i'd hardly slept
    he sent me home once more
& told me to add sleeping tablets
to the mix

two days later when i was
dangerously dizzy
    like dad when he was drunk
& disorderly
    i drove myself to the public
hospital

some people said to me later
i was silly & should have
called an ambulance
    but i'm not in the ambulance
fund
    & i didn't have money for a
taxi
    & i'm an independent
bastard too

after a near side-swipe to
a neighbour's car just
a hundred metres from home
    i sat up pretty quick —
thinking of the thickness of a coat
of paint
    & i rolled the windows down
& caught the breeze
    it was a slow five k drive

after a few minutes in the emergency
waiting room i thought i was going
to fall off the chair
    so i asked to lie on a
stretcher
    a man with a grey flecked beard
came across & spoke
    he told me they were reserved for
sick people & i should stay in my chair
    i told him he'd be sick if he didn't
wheel the stretcher over for me NOW

after i'd lain down he leaned over me
& said
    you'll have to get off if anyone
comes in who really needs it
    i suggested he'd better be able to
fight if he thought i'd be getting off

it only took another five hours & i was
moved in to see the second doctor
    when he saw how awkward i was —
& noticed how long it took me to sit
upright
    & saw i hadn't shaved for a week —

& heard my slurred speech
    he folded his arms & told me to go
home    have a sleep    & go back & see
that first doctor

i told him to get fucked
    met his eyes —
& said that if he didn't look at me
properly
    i'd spread him over the floor

after a look & a feel he sent me
for a CAT scan

when i returned he said
    i've called in a specialist —
you might have to wait for an hour
or so because he's coming from
another hospital

when i saw the third doctor he said
    you are very sick —
you have an infected abscess
& it's very close to the voice box
    you'll need to go into a bed
upstairs
    you may need an operation
in the morning

when they got me installed upstairs
i saw the fourth doctor
    he said —
you'd better prepare yourself
    this could be the big c

i thought i'd already met the big c
when i saw that second doctor

in the morning i met the fifth doctor
    a woman —
who one day later told me i did have
cancer
    but the way she told me
made me think she was the big c
    the lady doctor told me to go
home   she said they'd ring me
with a time to go to another hospital
    to see another doctor

after a week when no one had rung
    i rang the hospital

i spoke to a sixth doctor who told me
they never said they would ring me
    he said i was confused —
& that i should wait for a phone call
    or a letter

i told the sixth doctor that maybe
he was confused
    i said i remembered what
i'd been told

he said
    no   you are confused
we will tell you when we want to see
you
    & we'll do that by letter or phone —
whatever suits us best
    if you don't like it —
you know what to do
    you can go private & call the tune
& have doctors suit your timetable

i reminded the sixth doctor
i was a public patient & had no
private cover
   but i told him too i was
an old fashioned bloke

i said
   i'll keep an eye on the letterbox
& an ear out for the phone
   but i'll go outside every hour
& check the roof for homing pigeons
   so feel free to send your instructions
by carrier pigeon
   i've got a long ladder & a seventeen
foot high wall & i feel quite confident
i can climb the ladder & open up the
metal band    & retrieve any messages
you might like to send
   i'm happy to use the old technology —
or the new    i'll leave it up to you

the sixth doctor suggested we end the call

with respect    i said
   maybe i am confused & i don't really
have cancer
   can you confirm that i actually do
have cancer

yes    he replied    you do

& can you confirm that i did have an
ultra sound examination

yes   he replied   you did

& while i freely admit i don't have much
medical knowledge
   i do have a good understanding
of the nuances of language & speech
   & i do believe when the ultra sound
examination was carried out
   there was a good deal of surprise in
the voices of the five or six people
behind me in that darkened room
   would you agree on that point

yes   he replied   i agree

& while i don't want to appear pedantic
   would you agree that four   or perhaps
even five biopsy samples were removed
during that examination
   i'm sure i do remember the pull on the
flesh
   & i'm sure i heard instructions
on how deep to go   one point five
centimetetres   two centimetres
etcetera   etcetera
   i mean i won't argue on the number
of biopsies or the depth of the needles
   it's the procedure i'm referring to —
would you agree that i did in fact have several
biopsy samples taken

yes    he replied    i agree

well    thank you    i said
    i'll keep an eye on the letterbox
    an ear out for the phone
    & i'll check the roof hourly
thank you doctor for your decency
    your humanity
            & your kindness

& we both hung up

after a few more weeks i got to meet
the seventh doctor    a surgeon
    a decent bloke who showed me
decency & got it in return
    he explained my condition
in a language i could understand
    his handshake was as solid as
his eye contact & i liked his style

the seventh doctor had me lie on the
operating table for a biopsy
on my tongue because they couldn't
locate my primary
    the cancer in my neck was a secondary

on the day of the op he & his team all wore
blue overalls     white gumboots
caps & masks
    they looked like concrete finishers
on a building site
    but their hands were soft & their vowels
were rounded

before i was sent off to sleep
the seventh doctor talked to me
about painting
    & Robert Hannaford —
& poetry     & art as therapy
    he sure didn't sound like
a concrete finisher

when i awoke i was put into a ward of
other old men who coughed all night
& kept one another awake
    & when the screen curtains were
drawn in the morning
    i asked the man alongside me
if he'd like a Rothmans Plain

in his morning haze he couldn't fathom
my joke

later that morning i met a tribe of surgical
doctors who told me to go home
    my results would take five days
to process

but at six o'clock that night i had
to go back
    the abscess had started to swell
again
    & i met doctor eight

he arranged my re-admission & i was
given a different bed in the same ward
& dripped with antibiotics

when i awoke in the morning my chin
was a mass of sores
    & my bottom lip looked as though
it had been pumped with botox

doctors nine & ten came to see me after
i asked the nurse to get me a doctor
    but they were completely baffled

they didn't seem to be much older than
my teenage daughter
    & when they started mentioning the
possibility of a staf infection
    the nurse looked really alarmed

doctor nine suggested to doctor ten
they should go & look in their books to
see if they could identify the problem

when they left i told the nurse i'd like
to see a grown-up doctor
    i was scared     & so was she

when she came back with doctor eleven
she told him she'd like to move me from
the ward to a private room

doctor eleven said he didn't deem that
necessary
    he suggested it was maybe school sores

i suggested it might be cold sores
    but doctor eleven couldn't agree

i said i wanted to see a specialist
    it was a teaching hospital
& they must have someone capable of
an accurate diagnosis

by the time doctor twelve arrived the
nurse had panicked & moved me to
a private room
    i repeated to doctor twelve
i thought it might be cold sores due to
stress
    but he couldn't agree either

the following morning a tribe of surgical
doctors looked at me
    & no one seemed too sure

it was then that doctor thirteen came
to my bedside & cut the heads off
some of the pustules & swabbed me

days later    when the results finally arrived
    the spread had really increased
& the lip grown larger
    & i did in fact have cold sores —
but they called it herpes simplex virus

two days later they sent me home
with a bottle of Condy's crystals
    & packets of anti viral tabs

about two weeks further down the track
i met doctor fourteen    a dental doctor
    the split corners of my mouth were
still healing but she needed to inspect my
gums & teeth before my neck dissection
the next day
    i asked her to be careful    said i
didn't have a big mouth
    (although i'm sure some doctors
[& others] would dispute that)
    but she treated me with care —
stating that i did have a small opening
(& though i enjoy puns    i said nothing)
    her advice was to get a tube of
Daktarin cream & use it overnight
    but more importantly —
to smear it over the corners of my mouth
just prior to the operation
    she said it would be likely to stop
any cold sores from coming back
    & she was right

that next morning i saw doctor seven
again    in the same operating theatre
    he had his tribe of surgical doctors to
back him up along with two anaesthetists
& a few nurses
    as i was wheeled in
my eyes scanned for familiar faces
    doctor eight was smiling broadly
so i winked at him
    he understood my style & his smile
broadened

a couple of days later doctor eight
told me the surgical team had read
some of my poetry aloud as i was going
off
    that was doctor seven's idea

doctor eight said they'd stopped because
some of it seemed a little 'R' rated
    he said that after some of my lines
were read he remembered hearing me read
when he was a teenager at St Peter's College
    i remarked that it must have been
during Ray Stanley's reign
    when the school was a bit more liberal —
& more than just one voice was heard

he laughed at that
                    & i laughed too

i wasn't laughing when i woke up from
the neck dissection though
    it was 5:20pm when i sighted the clock
in the intensive care unit & i was feeling
cranky
    squinting    wondering where my glasses
were    & trying to calculate how long i'd been
lying there    & did they know i was awake

at 7:30pm they wheeled me back to the ward
    the same one i'd been in before    but again —
a different berth

& there to greet me was my girlfriend
& my youngest son Paul
    we counted backwards & calculated
it must have been a long operation

they said the wound looked like i'd
been carved up with a broken flagon
they said a bottle would have been
far too small    they said it looked scary —
& because i couldn't see what
my visitors saw
i asked a nurse for a mirror

it scared me too

by 9pm though i was asking for food
as much to my own surprise as that of
my visitors
but the swallowing wasn't fun

doctor seven had cut me from the bottom
of my left earlobe
to the top of my collarbone
then curled around & up to my adam's apple
it was a cut as big as a baling hook
& with its thirty metal staples
it looked almost as shiny & nearly as
dangerous

he'd performed his surgery on Holy Thursday
20th March 2008
& with the neck muscle removed he'd
left a hole    but he'd taken the tumour too
(intact we hope)    & with two previous
infections it had been quite a messy job

he was back at my bedside on Good Friday
morning    away from his own four kids
    explaining that i'd gone through the
easy part of the treatment
    that the chemo & the radiation were
to come in about six weeks
    after the wound had healed

he told me to go home & get into
the full cream milk    the banana smoothies
    all the chocolate i could eat    & anything else
that took my fancy & was fattening
    to get some weight on because i'd sure
as hell get it stripped off in six weeks time
    he told me too that my voice box had been
welded to the tumour
    that he'd had to cut it free & there'd
been some nerve damage & my voice mightn't
improve a lot on what i had at that point
    but i was still talking
& i was still listening
    grateful to have doctor seven on my side

it was a good Friday to get that news
    i lay in bed eating Easter eggs —
silver paper & cellophane
surrounding me
    chocolate    sliding down my throat.

## Ideas for transformation

# The Seventh Doctor

Geoff felt he wasn't treated with basic humanity until he met 'The Seventh Doctor', the ENT surgeon who looked after Geoff with excellent medical skills, brilliant communication skills and a wonderful bedside manner. 'The Seventh Doctor' is an account of one man's experience in the public health system, particularly of the lack of choice and freedom one may have as a public patient. Geoff uses humour throughout the poem to counter the often bleak subject matter, showing us how to laugh in the face of adversity.

## Transformation Task 1: Radio Script

### Challenging Authority

Geoff encountered a distinct lack of respect from a number of professionals in the public health system. The Seventh Doctor stopped and listened to him respectfully, recognising that he had genuine grievances, and responding accordingly. For many people self-advocating can be extremely difficult. Working class people are often intimidated by class barriers and don't have the language skills to understand, let alone argue, with their doctor. Migrants and refugees may face the same dilemma. Create a radio script that delves into the public health system, focusing on the numbers-driven approach to treatment. Listen to an episode of 'Background Briefing' on ABC Radio National **www.abc.net.au/radionational/programs/backgroundbriefing**

## Transformation Task 2: Monologue

### Humour in Adversity

A cancer diagnosis is no laughing matter. It is a testament to Geoff's character that he was able to use humour, sarcasm and wit in the face of such adversity. In fact laughing in the face of adversity is a common practice among working class Australians. Write a monologue that explores a situation where the character uses humour to deal with a challenging experience.

## Transformation Task 3: Webpage

### The Rights of People

'The Seventh Doctor' is a critique of the public health system and a passionate call for the rights of people to fair and respectful treatment. Each and every one of us deserves respect, whichever side of the counter we happen to be on. Sickness makes us vulnerable physically and emotionally. While hospitals are places of healing they can also be places of tension and drama, for staff as well as patients.

Of rising concern is the amount of violence that emergency services personnel and emergency department staff experience, often as a result of Methamphetamine and alcohol abuse, but also exacerbated by long waiting times at hospitals due to government cost-cutting measures. In 2016 the SA Health Minister reported that in the last three years ambulance officers had experienced a seventy-four percent increase in violent incidents.

Create an online web campaign that advocates for the rights of emergency department staff, paramedics, police officers and SES personnel to work safely.

# Hamming It Up

## Themes

Growing Up
Childhood Memories
Parenting

## Text Types

Persuasive Speech
Biography
Letter

Geoff Goodfellow's context statement for:

## Hamming It Up

This story is set in the mid-1950s when Australia was still divided by sectarianism. My family were Catholics and we were well aware of the Protestants around us with whom we were vying for dominance. Church services in my Catholic parish drew around 300 people for the eight am service with around the same number for ten am. The Mass was said in Latin to people who would dress in their best set of clothes. Most people lived in homes on a quarter-acre block with fruit trees and a chook shed. Pubs and shops weren't open on Sundays and it was generally considered a family day.

In this story I wanted to share a child's-eye view of suburban life in 1950s Australia. I wanted to take my readers into an era that is largely unrecognisable today to those who are under forty.

My story begins in our large suburban backyard and moves through our neighbourhood, describing moments of simple pleasure in my little boy's voice. I wanted to show my father's cheeky sense of humour in the interactions he had, not only with me, but also with others during our walk. I also wanted to show how aware I was of the significance of the conversation I overheard between my dad and our near neighbour.

Even though we only went to the local public telephone box for him to make a call, it was exciting for me to get this one-to-one time with my dad, and the events of that morning are stencilled into my memory.

# Hamming It Up

It was a Sunday morning in 1956 and we'd just got home from eight am Mass. I changed out of my good clothes and put on a pair of shorts, a tee-shirt and my school sandals. Mum and Dad were drinking a pot of tea in the kitchen and reading the paper when I walked out the back door, careful not to let the screen door slam. It was already quite warm and the backyard with all its fruit trees seemed a cooler place to be. Besides that, whilst I'd been kneeling down that morning, not understanding any of the Latin Father Killian was using, I'd been thinking about the one peach that was still left up on the tree. I'd spotted it when I was in the chook shed getting the eggs before church. It was high up and was going to be hard to get, but it didn't look as though the birds had beaten me to it.

I dragged an empty banana box out of the shed, across the yard, then up-ended it below the peach tree. It was a white peach, its fruit really fleshy and juicy with smooth and furry skin dusted with tinges of soft pink. This last one looked like the best one too. I got the yard broom out of the shed and climbed on top of the box. I pushed the broom head up through a tangle of branches to try and tap it gently so it might drop. I knew I'd have to be quick then to catch it without falling off the box and hurting myself. But I was just a little bit too short to reach it. If the box had been six inches higher I could have got it for sure. My best chance now was to scale the tree on one of the biggest branches and try to reach out for it. I'd just started to get really close when I heard the slap of the screen door closing, then Dad's voice yelling out, *Geoff, where are ya?*

*Up here*, I replied, but he could hardly see me because the apricot and the nectarine trees were between us. I could see him though, but I was fairly high up and I could see he was looking for me on the ground.

*I'm up in the peach tree*, I yelled.

*What the bloody hell are you doin' up there?*

*There's one peach left and I'm tryin' to get it*, I explained.

He wandered down and got directly underneath me. *You hop down and I'll get the ladder and get it for ya. Now c'mon, hop down before ya fall down.*

By the time I'd climbed down he was back with the wooden step ladder and started to position it so it was really steady. He asked me to stand side-on to the ladder and hold onto it with both hands. He had to get right up on the very top step too, and I could feel the ladder start to rock a little bit. He must've felt it too because he said, *You keep a firm hold on it. I don't want to go arse up.*

*I've got it,* I said, and tightened my grip a bit more.

*I've got it too,* he said, *and it's a bloody beauty.* And then he started to descend. When he got back down he passed it to me. It was perfect, apart from one little spot where a bird had stuck its beak in for a taste. That didn't worry me though, I got straight into it. Soon I had peach juice all over my chin and dripping from my fingers. Those damn peaches were so tasty.

Dad came back from putting the ladder and the box back in the shed and said, *When ya finished eating that, go to the bathroom, wash your face and hands, and you can come out for a walk with me.*

*Sure,* I said. I'd just turned seven and I hardly ever went out for a walk just with him. When I asked if Anne or Mark were coming too, he said, *Naw, it's just you an' me.*

*Where we goin'?* I asked.

*Go an' have a wash an' I'll tell ya.*

When I came back out he said, *Don't get too excited. We're just goin' around to Collins Street to use the public phone. But if you behave ya self, you can drop the four pennies in and press the button for me. Can ya do that?*

*Easy.*

We had about a quarter of a mile to where the phone box was. After we'd turned the first corner, John Rowe's dog, a black and white mongrel, ran alongside the inside of their front fence growling at us. Dad growled back at the dog and it started barking. Dad started barking too, and I was laughing, telling him to do it some more, but he wouldn't. A bit further on we met Mrs Parker. She was on her way back from the deli. She peeled open the packet of Craven A's she'd just bought and they stood there on the footpath, having a smoke. She told Dad she was worried about her husband Jack losing his licence 'cos he's just been pinched for drunk driving. Jack was a cab driver and she said she didn't know what they'd do after his licence was taken. Dad didn't have his licence either, now. That's why we were walking up to the phone box. He'd already been caught twice, I knew that.

After we turned into Robert Avenue we could see the corner deli up on our left and I knew the phone box was just around the corner. Sometimes I used to go up to the deli on my own to get Dad a packet of Rothmans Plain. He always let me get an ice cream cone with the change.

*Can ya get me an ice cream at the shop please Dad?*

First up he said, *Little boys that ask for things don't get any, and little boys that don't ask for things, don't want any.* After a long pause he said, *Your best bet is to say nothing.*

But then he started smiling and said, *Yeah, course you can have an ice cream, but I'll make the phone call first.*

When we turned the corner and got to the phone box there was a lady inside it already. We stood alongside the phone box in the sun, waiting for her to finish. She knew we were there and kept turning around and looking at us before turning away again. But she just kept talking anyway. Ten minutes later she was still going. When she turned the next time Dad caught her eye through the glass panel and started making out to reel in a fishing line. But the lady just turned away and carried on talking. She was still doing the same thing five minutes later.

*C'mon*, Dad said, and I thought we were going home. Instead, we went into the corner deli. The bell jangled on the door when we went in and the owner came out to serve us. Dad asked if he could make me up a single cone of vanilla and the bloke winked at me and went to it straight away. While he was scooping it out, Dad said we'd been waiting on the phone for about twenty minutes. Then he walked across and looked out the shop window and said she was still going. *She'll get laryngitis*, Dad said, and the man laughed. After Dad paid the man he asked him if he could do him a favour. The bloke then passed over a tinned ham that was sitting up on the shelf behind him.

*Shouldn't be much more than a minute*, Dad said, and I followed him out and back around the corner to the phone box door. He knocked a couple of times then opened the door and said, *I've brought this tinned ham out for ya. Ya must be starting to get hungry in there by now.*

The lady was off the phone in about ten seconds flat and stormed off down Collins Street, away from us, muttering, but we couldn't quite hear what she was saying.

Dad took the ham back into the shop then and the bloke was at the side window, still laughing. He had tears in his eyes and said, *That's the funniest bloody thing I've seen since I opened the shop.*

Dad made his phone call and we walked home, talking about the lady. I remember Mum laughing like mad when Dad told her what happened. She really loved it when Dad was playful. You could tell by her laugh.

## Ideas for transformation

# Hamming It Up

'Hamming It Up' invokes happy memories of growing up in Adelaide in the fifties. Some of our most evocative writing comes out of early childhood experiences. Over time we can look back and see clearly how we have been shaped by the events of our early life. Particular memories can provide springboards for great writing.

## Transformation Task 1: Persuasive Speech

### Growing up

'Hamming It Up' provides insights into growing up in the fifties, when Sunday Mass was an integral part of family and community life, backyards were large and filled with fruit trees, pennies were needed to use the public phone and life moved more slowly. Growing up today is very different for young people – but is it better? Write a persuasive speech: 'Growing up in the fifties would be better than growing up in Australia today.'

## Transformation Task 2: Biography

### Childhood Memories

Geoff has written about a simple childhood memory that gives insight into the kind of man his father was. Interview one of your parents or another significant adult about an important memory from their childhood. Write a biography that explores the significance of the memory for that person.

## Transformation Task 3: Letter

### Parenting

'Hamming It Up' expresses the joy Geoff felt spending time alone with his dad. The story is autobiographical. A transformation could be to write this experience from the perspective of Geoff's father. What might his thoughts and feelings be about these moments spent with his son? What are his hopes and fears for his child? What does he want his son to know about him and about the world? Write a letter from Geoff's dad to his son exploring aspects of the story that are not told, such as Geoff's father's ideas about being a man, a husband and a parent.

# What Harry Taught Me

## Themes

The Value of Work

Immigration

The Role of Mentors

## Text Types

Play Script

Letter

Poem

Geoff Goodfellow's context statement for:

## What Harry Taught Me

This is an insider's account of working class life in a butcher shop in mid-sixties Adelaide.

Working class life is not often the subject matter of novels, short stories or poetry.

I was fifteen years of age and working as an apprentice butcher for Turner's, a company with a chain of butcher shops scattered around Adelaide. I'd grown up in the northern suburbs with mainly Anglo-Celtic culture although I had school friends who were the sons of migrants. My working life introduced me to migrant men who were the face of cultural change in post-war Australia. At Turner's I met Harry, a Latvian man who set about teaching me a set of work skills that would equip me to be eminently employable. Not only work skills though.

In many respects, Harry became my mentor and provided me with a model which was often in sharp contrast to the dominant Australian male culture of the time. He had impeccable dress sense, was exacting and precise in his work, and didn't allow his drinking to interfere with his work life. He taught me to observe closely – and I had to learn to listen carefully due to his accent.

In the front of the butcher shop, behind the counter, I was absorbing the innuendo practised on the largely female customers by the all-male staff. Out the back of the butcher shop, Harry was introducing me to the inside jokes of the butchering trade, with 'summer lamb' being a prime example of how to be playful with language.

The morality Harry was proposing to me was somewhat questionable. He was full of ambiguity. No drinking during working hours, no cheeky innuendo on the counter, but always make sure you press a finger down on the scales and overcharge any customer who dares mess up your display by selecting the best cuts.

## What Harry Taught Me

For a butcher, Harry was a classic dresser, in the traditional European sense. He was in his late forties when we met and I was just a kid. Harry had been in Australia for only a handful of years when we began working together in 1965. He was the first Latvian I'd ever met and he captivated me with his style and old-fashioned mannerisms. He was so different from Mike, a fourth generation Australian and the shop manager, and nothing at all like Frank, a little Cockney bloke who spent most of his time on the counter, charming the ladies with his rhyming slang and clever use of language. Dick and Terry were the backroom butchers, both a couple of knock-a-bouts, more likely to read a newspaper than a novel. Harry always wore a crisp white shirt with a black bow tie under his white butcher's coat and striped apron. His jet black hair was slicked down and he had a pencil-line moustache that looked as though it had been drawn on. I was fifteen-and-a-half but I'd never seen anyone who looked like Harry, except perhaps in a black and white movie. He had a really heavy accent and within minutes of meeting me nicknamed me *Sviveldash*.

I asked him why he chose to call me that. What did it mean?

*Don' vurry vai*, he said, *from now on, yoo are Sviveldash, en zat iz all zere iz to it. Now get mi a rump en za clin tray Sviveldash. Don' muk aroun. I tri to tich yoo sumsing.*

Mike had told me earlier that afternoon that I was to be Harry's gofer. It was only on Thursday nights that Harry and I would work together, during a preliminary introduction to late night shopping in outer suburban Adelaide. I worked for Turner's Butchers at the Clovercrest Shopping Centre in Modbury, a newly developed suburb of mainly first home buyers with double income households, but with quite a few pram pushers too. The trial proved to be a great success and Turner's was as busy as a tin full of worms every Thursday night. There were six of us working the shop through the week but on that one night we had another seven butchers working the floor until nine o'clock. Turner's had around a dozen shops scattered around Adelaide and the extra blokes would come in by six from a variety of different locations. A couple of them would always stop off and belt a few quick pints down before arriving, often lobbing in a little unsteady on their feet. And the peppermints they chewed on gave them right away. Behind the counter with a few beers under their belt, their chatter with the ladies sometimes got overly risqué, their innuendo far too strong. After a few weeks, one young woman's husband arced up and Mike had to tell both blokes to pull up on their drinking or they'd be off the roster. Harry laughed his head off when he heard Mike had given them a serve. He said, *Zay are clowns. Hev no respek for any**sing** or any**vun**.* Moments later he told me, *I alvays vait til I get home en zen I hev mi vodka.* Meeting people like Harry sure made me think about how different my culture was from his. I didn't know anyone else then who drank vodka.

Harry and I enjoyed each other's company and we worked well together. Early on the third night he said, *Lissen Sviveldash, yoo don' von to be bak room butcher braking up za beef en doing za hard vurk. Yoo shood be shop butcher. I vill teach yoo to vindow dress. I am za bess. I can make ezy yor life.*

Harry came out from the main city shop where he was regarded as the best window dresser in Adelaide. No-one disputed his ability to dress a stainless steel tray with style and flair. Mike was grateful for Harry's contribution on Thursday nights and knew I was picking up valuable skills under Harry's guidance. I was quick off the mark to grab a forequarter or loin of lamb, a topside or a rump, or whatever Harry was calling for . . . and attentive as Harry trimmed off the excess, observing that he always left a neat selvedge of clean white fat for presentation. Harry told me numerous times, *Yoo muss hev za red . . . en za vite.* I'd witness, too, the concentration and effort he put into the art of placement – every move was considered. Harry taught me to save the prime slices for the front and top and to always bury the poorer cuts on the underside at the back of the tray.

One night as I came back from placing a tray of rump in the window display, Mike said, *Tell Harry to send out a tray of porterhouse after the summer lamb chops.* As Harry was putting the final touches to the lamb by adding a couple of sprigs of parsley, I asked him why they called it summer lamb.

Harry winked and said, *Summa **lamb**. . . en summa **hogget**. Now qvick, go Sviveldash. Tek out zis tray vile I cut za porterhouse. En pleze, fine out vot zey vont nex.*

I came back out, grabbing a full topside from the rack in the cool room. Harry was sharpening his steak knife on the steel as I lay the topside on the wooden block. He went straight to work on it, trimming it and observing it from a few angles. By the time I'd got a fresh tray, he'd started slicing it and was soon laying out the slices.

*Sviveldash, votch me. Yoo ken lern. Rememba . . . za customer iz alvays standing at za frunt of za tray. Alvays dress za tray from za frunt. En Sviveldash, if yoo are serving za customer en za customer vonts yor top layer, or za peece rite at za frunt, make shore yoo rest vun finger on za scales ven yoo veigh for price. Fuck zem. If zay fuck up yor display, yoo make zem pay. Zis is za only vay. Lern it.*

## Ideas for transformation

# What Harry Taught Me

'What Harry Taught Me' reflects on the role of mentors in our lives. The story conveys a deep sense of gratitude and respect for Harry and the lessons learnt under his tutelage, even if Harry's ethics were at times a little questionable. Who are the mentors in your life? What are the important lessons you have learnt?

## Transformation Task 1: Play Script

### The Importance of Work

In this story, working in the butcher shop is something of a rite of passage for the teenage Geoff. Harry taught Geoff valuable lessons including how to present yourself, who to listen to, how to relate to a variety of people and the need to excel in your work. He also instructed him in the importance of self-discipline, self-respect and the need to show respect where it is due.

Write a play script that highlights a key moment when you began to understand the importance of work, whether at school, at home or in the workforce.

## Transformation Task 2: Letter

### Immigration

'What Harry Taught Me' highlights the ways immigrants contribute to the fabric of Australian society. Statistics show immigrants make an immediate and significant contribution to Australian society, economically and culturally. Immigration is a contentious topic in Australia. Write a letter to the Minister for Immigration expressing your support for allowing more immigrants to settle in Australia. Use information from Geoff's story to support your claims. You may also want to choose a recent news story or opinion piece to assist you with your letter.

## Transformation Task 3: Poem

### The Role of Mentors

Harry was a significant mentor for Geoff. The respect and warmth Geoff felt for Harry is evident throughout this story. In describing Harry, Geoff highlights the cultural differences that intrigue him but also the firm but fair way Harry goes about teaching him the skillset required to be a window dresser in a butcher shop.

'What Harry Taught Me' culminates in a questionable aspect of Harry's character. In some ways this surprising aspect endears Harry to us even more.

Think of a person you consider to be your mentor; it may be an aunt/uncle, a family friend or a teacher. Write a poem about this person and what you have learnt from them. Consider their individual personality traits, mannerisms and qualities.

# Don't Look So Glum

## The Writer's Statement

What is a Writer's Statement?

The Transformed Text 'Don't Look So Glum'

Exemplar of a Writer's Statement

## What is a Writer's Statement?

For assessment purposes the Transformation Task may require the production of a Writer's Statement to accompany the transformed text. In the opening chapter I used the analogy of home renovation shows as a way to describe the concept of transformation. While the final reveal of the transformed house is important, the essence of the show is in the weeks of documentation about the process taken to get there. The audience follows the renovators as they make choices about walls, paint, flooring, lighting, cabinetry, furniture. In the same way, the Writer's Statement for a Transformation Task is a record of the choices made by a student regarding form, purpose, language, audience and context in the process of creating a new text.

There are three main components in a well-structured Writer's Statement:

- Firstly, the Writer's Statement needs to identify the text type, audience and themes of the original text and specify which elements will be maintained in the transformed text. This is an opportunity for students to demonstrate their thorough understanding of the 'springboard' text and its context.
- Secondly, the Writer's Statement should identify the text type, audience and themes of the new transformed text. Students must explain what text type/genre they have created, who they have created it for and how the transformed text is connected to the context, structure and ideas of the original text.
- Finally, the Writer's Statement needs to identify the stylistic features and techniques used to convey the themes/ideas to the audience of the transformed text. Students must name the specific techniques they have employed and provide examples from their transformed text. Their analysis should also discuss how those techniques shape meaning and position the target audience.

‘Don’t Look So Glum’ is Geoff’s transformation of one of his best known poems, ‘Don’t Call Me Lad’. Accompanying the transformed text is an example of a Writer’s Statement that discusses the connections between the ‘springboard’ text and the newly created text. Geoff has chosen to use the form, structure and themes of the original poem to create a new poem for an entirely new audience.

## Don't Look So Glum

Don't look so glum mum
    don't look so glum
was that a finger
or a thumb mum
    don't look so glum

i've been out having fun mum
    yeah out havin' fun
don't poke out your tongue mum
    don't look so glum

my homework is done mum
    stop wavin' y'r gun
all assignments are done mum
    don't look so glum

you're old & i'm young mum
    your best days are done
dad's been gone f'r five years mum
    don't look so glum

yeah i've tattooed my bum mum
    & put a stud through my tongue
it's not the end of the world mum
    don't look so glum

i don't do hard drugs mum
    i go to parties for fun
so get off my case mum
    don't look so glum

sure my skirt's a bit short mum
    but you can't see my bum
don't nag me again mum
    i'm dressed to have fun

i practise safe sex mum
   i'm not particularly dumb
i get love & respect mum
   don't look so glum

it's a mad crazy world mum
   & i need to have fun
year twelve is a drag mum
   three months & it's done
yeah   leave me alone mum
   three months & it's done.

## Writer's Statement for *Don't Look So Glum*

The published text 'Don't Call Me Lad' conveys the angst of a teenage boy who is striving to find his own identity, voice, and position as he moves towards adulthood. In the poem he metaphorically spars with his father, taunting and antagonising him, and in the process articulates sentiments with which many young men would readily identify. The transformed poem 'Don't Look So Glum' has been written as a sister poem to 'Don't Call Me Lad' in order to explore similar conflict teenage girls may engage in with their mothers.

**Introductory sentence reveals awareness of the tone and ideas of original text.**

**A clear introduction to the nature of the transformation task.**

The target audience of 'Don't Look So Glum' is young women, and the purpose of the poem is to directly address the conflict many girls experience with their mothers as they begin asserting their power and claiming more autonomy. I wanted young women to recognise themselves in the poem and for the poem to validate their struggle for independence.

**Highlights audience and purpose of transformed text so that the following analysis is contextualised.**

The imperative title 'Don't Look So Glum' foreshadows the conflict as the teenage daughter is telling her mother what to do, in fact she is telling her mother off. It is the same language often heard, loaded with irritation and resentment, between mothers and daughters in suburban homes as tensions rise. Its tone is both a complaint and a taunt. I used the adjective glum as a keyword throughout the poem, not just because it rhymes well with mum, but because it is evocative of facial expression, posture and body language. This visual imagery sets the scene and particularly highlights the mother's unhappiness and her disapproval of her daughter's choices.

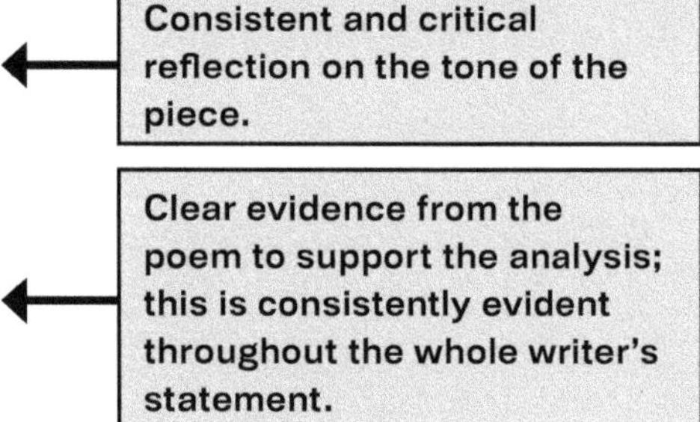


In 'Don't Look So Glum' I have maintained

some stylistic techniques, structures and themes from 'Don't Call Me Lad', but have adopted the voice of a seventeen-year-old girl. The free verse form of 'Don't Call Me Lad' has been retained, with mostly four-line stanzas, and repetition of the title phrase in almost every stanza. Structuring the poem this way echoes the rhythm and rhyme of 'Don't Call Me Lad' and recreates the feeling of the parent being repeatedly, verbally repelled. This feeling is reinforced in 'Don't Call Me Lad' through the use of an ABAB rhyme scheme. In 'Don't Look So Glum' I have employed a mono-rhyme scheme, with repeating end-words such as, *mum, bum* and *glum*. The short rhyming vowel sound 'u' and recurring consonant 'm' in these words create a percussive assonance which further magnifies the feeling of verbal hammering. The rhythmic and musical effects of these combined techniques make both poems catchy and easy to commit to memory.

Colloquial language is used throughout 'Don't Call Me Lad' and I have maintained this feature in 'Don't Look So Glum'. Classic teenage lines such as, *so get off my case mum*, are likely to draw an emotive response from the teenage target audience, as are the rude and obscene gestures in, *was that a finger/or a thumb mum*, and, *don't poke out your tongue mum*. Disrespectful and confrontational statements like, it's not the end of the world mum, and, don't nag me again mum, further develop the antagonistic tone while accurately portraying the kind of conflict played out between many teenagers and their parents. Experimentation with drugs and sex is addressed in stanzas six and eight with the lines, *i don't do hard drugs mum,* and, *i practise safe sex mum*. Inclusion of these iconic issues reflects the real life concerns of many teenage girls and their mothers.

**Understanding of the conventions of the text type.**

**Analysis of the structure of the poem in order to enhance the tone.**

**Perceptive analysis of the use of poetic techniques such as rhyme and assonance in order to create an intense atmosphere.**

**Explains the purpose of using colloquial language in order to heighten the sense of conflict.**

**Language and tone draws in the audience by making reference to elements of shared experience.**

**Clear examples from the poem of colloquial language reinforce the analysis.**

**Clear evidence from the text supports the rationale for the 'antagonistic tone'.**

As a male writer representing a female relationship in 'Don't Look So Glum' it was important that I did not imbue the poem with an overly masculine voice. I decided to represent the girl with a more controlled kind of anger than the boy in 'Don't Call Me Lad'. His anger could be described as 'punchy' whereas hers might be described as 'snarky'. This portrayal might be considered gender stereotyping, however I needed a way to make the girl's voice distinctly female, and have used words and phrases given to me by teenage girls and their mothers. The anger, aggression and sarcasm in 'Don't Call Me Lad' is overtly masculine as the boy attacks his father's virility with the taunt, *got more hair on my balls dad/than y'v got/or had*. In 'Don't Look So Glum' the perceived loss of sexual attractiveness in women as they age is used by the girl against her mother as an insulting taunt in the same vein: *you're old & i'm young mum/your best days are done/dad's been gone f'r five years mum/don't look so glum*.

**Explains how the writer's personal involvement in writing the text, impacted the final piece and adds credibility to the authenticity of the task.**

**Clear line of reasoning in order to position the reader as to why language choices were made.**

**Clear rationale for the sustained focus of intensity of the verbal assault through the examples from the monologue.**

The teenage girl I have portrayed in 'Don't Look So Glum' does not buy into the patriarchal imperative that women must be 'good': quiet, compliant, pleasing, pretty, sexually attractive but not sexually active or empowered. I have placed her in first person so that she speaks for herself, asserting her power vocally throughout the poem in lines such as: *i'm not particularly dumb, all assignments are done*, and, *i need to have fun*. Stanzas five and seven describe how she also asserts her power physically in the world through tattooing, piercing and dressing her body as she wishes, with, *yeah i've tattooed my bum mum/& put a stud through my tongue*, and, *sure my skirt's a bit short mum/but you can't see my bum*. Stanza eight further supports the suggestion she is comfortable and confident

**Consistent use of sophisticated language and concepts.**

**Evidence of use of first person perspective as a stylistic feature to sustain her assertive stance toward her mother.**

**Use of contemporary contentious issues for young adults as part of the content of the poem helps reinforce the key ideas regarding identity and intended target audience.**

**By continuing to refer to various stanzas, it reveals a sustained development of argument and analysis of the transformation task.**

with her sexuality in the lines, *i practise safe sex mum*, and, *i get love and respect mum.* I have used this characterisation to show a young woman who knows she is boss of her own body and mind, and who has faith in her own judgement about what is right for her. Even so, it is not difficult to imagine how a mother might find such attitudes and experimentation worrying and confronting.

Awareness of stylistic features evident in the continued use of techniques such as characterisation, rhyme, rhythm and imagery.

Like the boy in 'Don't Call Me Lad', the teenage girl in 'Don't Look So Glum' is her own person and no matter how painful the conflict, she knows she must push against her parent for more room to grow. My hope and intention in writing this poem is that young women will find it validating, amusing, satisfying and even transformative.

Solid resolution that reinforces the rationale for having written this transformation piece in light of the original.

# Support Materials

## Senior English: Creating Texts

**Student Task Sheets**

**& Proformas**

# Transformation Task

## Description of task:

This text production task involves taking a text and transforming it to produce a newly created and original text. The aim of the task is for you demonstrate a thorough and complex understanding of the ways in which the form and conventions of a text are significant in the making of meaning for an audience.

An example of a transformation is *Hamlet* into *The Lion King*. By updating the socio-cultural context of the 'springboard' text, a new and original text has been created. Elements such as the genre, form, structure and setting of the 'springboard' text have been changed while the characters, key themes and plot development remain the same in the transformed text.

To create a transformed text significant variations should be made to one or more elements of the 'springboard' text and can include changes to the genre, context, structure or stylistic features of the text. While the transformed text can be any text type, certain elements of the 'springboard' text need to be retained to demonstrate a connection between the texts.

## Assessment design criteria:

Assessment is based on the extent to which you are able to:

- demonstrate an awareness of how literary texts can be adapted to suit different audiences, purposes, times, places and perspectives
- analyse the relationship between original texts and the transformed text through the chosen alterations
- utilise a range of literary techniques and conventions for the chosen text type in order to create your transformed text
- review, edit and refine your created text for control of content, organisation, sentence structure, vocabulary and fluency

For assessment purposes the Transformation Task has two parts:

**Part 1: Transformation Text:** select a poem by Geoff Goodfellow to be transformed into another poem or text type. This task demonstrates that you have been able to transform and adapt the initial text in order to create an altered meaning.

**Choices for genre that your text can be transformed into:**

| | | | | |
|---|---|---|---|---|
| monologue | drama script | advertisement | review | graphic novel |
| cartoon | auto/biography | recount | diary | journal article |
| narrative | movie trailer | letter | blog | persuasive essay |
| web-page | song lyric | speech | opinion column | poem |
| news article | editorial | memoir | obituary | or … |

## Creating a Writer's Statement

**Part 2: Writer's Statement:** it is here that you articulate an awareness of the literary conventions of your chosen text type to support your interpretation. You need to detail why you have chosen the new text type and how the crafting of your new text and its stylistic features make an impact on your intended audience and the intended meaning.

The purpose of a Writer's Statement is to identify and discuss the choices you have made in crafting your transformed text. The Writer's Statement is an analysis of your own created text that identifies the form, structure, tone and literary techniques used to convey the themes/ideas to your chosen target audience. The structure and content of a Writer's Statement is dependent on the type of text you have chosen to create.

There are three key elements that need to be addressed:

- The text type and the target audience of both the original and transformed texts. This includes demonstrating your understanding of the purpose of both text types.
- The elements of the original text that you have maintained in your transformed text.
- The stylistic features used in your transformed text to convey the themes/ideas to your chosen target audience. These include the form and literary devices specific to the text type you have chosen. For example, columns in a newspaper article, first-person narrative perspective in a memoir or hyperbole in an opinion column.

### The Formula TER

When discussing the techniques you have employed in your transformed text the formula TER will help you to provide an appropriate level of analysis.

- T = Technique: Identify the technique you have employed in your text
- E = Example: Provide an example of the technique being used in your text
- R = Reflection: Explain how the technique effectively conveys the themes/ideas of your text type to your intended audience.

The 'Stylistic Features of Written/Visual Text Types' handout will assist you to accurately identify the techniques you have employed in your transformed text in order to create a thorough Writer's Statement.

# Stylistic Features of Written Text Types

| AUTO/BIOGRAPHY | ESSAY | JOURNAL ARTICLE | WEBPAGE |
|---|---|---|---|
| ***Autobiography: authors tell about events in their own lives***<br>***Biography: authors tell about events in the lives of others***<br>***Memoir: narrative based on a person's true life story***<br>Characterisation<br>Character interaction<br>Anecdotes<br>Setting<br>Narrative structure (includes flashbacks)<br>Poetic devices (alliteration /symbolism/motifs)<br>Dialogue<br>Narrative perspective | ***Essays are generally scholarly pieces of writing giving the author's own argument and supported by evidence***<br>Title/sub-headings<br>Main contention (issue, point)<br>Point of view<br>Tone<br>Structuring (engaging opening, developed middle, convincing ending)<br>Relevant/topical examples<br>Research and evidence (facts, statistics etc)<br>Style(s) of language (formal/subjective)<br>Personal anecdote<br>Contrast<br>Analogy<br>Persuasive language<br>Narrative structure (line of argument) | ***A formal and factual report aimed at informing the reader about a specific topic***<br>Point of view<br>Structure<br>Personal anecdote<br>Accompanying visuals (photos)<br>Expert opinion<br>Tone<br>Motif<br>Layout<br>Style(s) of language (formal/subjective)<br>Specific audience<br>Specific terminology/ jargon<br>Research and evidence (facts, statistics etc)<br>Diagrams, graphs and tables<br>Glossary of terms | ***A document, usually including hypertext, on the World Wide Web that incorporates text, graphics and sometimes sound***<br>Subjective language<br>Layout<br>First-person perspective<br>Research and evidence (facts, statistics etc)<br>Background/foreground<br>Accompanying visuals (moving/static, symbols/ icons)<br>Personal anecdotes<br>Title<br>Repetition<br>Hyperbole<br>Font (bold, size)<br>Colours<br>Specific audience<br>Diagrams, graphs and tables<br>Tone |
| **OPINION COLUMN** | **BLOG** | **EDITORIAL** | **PLAY SCRIPT** |
| ***An article created to reflect the author's subjective perspective/ view on a topic***<br>Bias<br>Tone<br>Expert opinion<br>Research and evidence (facts, statistics etc)<br>Anecdotal evidence<br>Rhetorical questions<br>Title<br>Hyperbole<br>First-person perspective<br>Relevant/topical examples<br>Style(s) of language (colloquial/sophisticated/ subjective) | ***A regularly updated website or webpage, typically run by an individual or small group, written in an informal or conversational style***<br>Subjective language<br>Layout<br>Structure<br>First-person perspective<br>Research and evidence (facts, statistics etc)<br>Accompanying visuals<br>Personal anecdotes<br>Title<br>Humorous tone<br>Repetition<br>Hyperbole<br>Font size<br>Colours<br>Specific audience | ***A newspaper article expressing the opinions/ beliefs of the editor towards topics of public debate***<br>Personal anecdote<br>Research and evidence (facts, statistics etc)<br>Poetic devices (alliteration /symbolism/ motifs)<br>Expert opinion<br>Pun<br>Style(s) of language (colloquial/inclusive/ subjective)<br>Hyperbole<br>Analogy<br>Relevant/topical examples | ***The printed text of a play or other dramatic composition; used in preparing for a performance***<br>Stage directions<br>Setting description<br>Sound/music cues<br>Dialogue<br>Narrative structure (Acts)<br>Narrative perspective<br>Introduction (context)<br>Monologues<br>Title<br>Breaking the fourth wall<br>Poetic devices (alliteration /symbolism/ motifs)<br>Costuming<br>Proxemics<br>Voice modulation<br>Props<br>Entrances and exits |

# Stylistic Features of Written Text Types

| REVIEW | SPEECH | NARRATIVE | POEM |
|---|---|---|---|
| ***A formal assessment of some text with the intention of improving it if possible***<br>Point of view<br>Structure<br>Anecdotal evidence<br>Setting<br>Imagery (visual, gustatory, olfactory)<br>Metaphor<br>Simile<br>Accompanying visuals<br>Adjectives<br>Rhetorical questions<br>Tone (approving, laudatory, dismissive, mocking, objective, subjective)<br>Genre of the review (e.g. reviewing a restaurant versus reviewing cars) | ***A formal address or discourse delivered to an audience***<br>Rhetorical questions<br>Anecdotal evidence<br>First-person perspective<br>Repetition<br>Facts/statistics<br>Humour<br>Hyperbole<br>Style(s) of language (inclusive/subjective)<br>Poetic devices (alliteration/symbolism/ motifs)<br>Narrative structure | ***A narrative is a spoken or written account of connected events; a story***<br>Title<br>Narrative structure<br>Narrative perspective<br>Imagery<br>Style(s) of language<br>Symbolism/ motifs<br>Characterisation<br>Setting<br>Character interaction<br>Metaphor<br>Simile<br>Dialogue<br>Tone<br>Contrast<br>Conflict | ***A text in which the expression of feelings and ideas is enhanced by devices such as rhyme, rhythm, and imagery***<br>Simile<br>Personification<br>Symbolism/motifs<br>Metaphor<br>Imagery (visual, aural)<br>Alliteration<br>Onomatopoeia<br>Assonance<br>Repetition<br>Rhythm<br>Form<br>Subjective language<br>Point of view<br>Setting<br>Structure<br>Title<br>Olfactory |

| EULOGY | OBITUARY | LETTER | FEATURE ARTICLE |
|---|---|---|---|
| ***A speech about a deceased person summarising their life, presented at a funeral ceremony***<br>Anecdotes<br>Dignified, respectful tone<br>Personal recollections<br>Structure<br>Quotations<br>Inclusive language<br>Appropriate humour<br>Expression of condolence<br>First-person perspective<br>Past tense | ***A short biography of a person who recently passed away, usually written by a person who knew the deceased. It is often published in a newspaper***<br>Biographical details<br>List of deceased person's accomplishments<br>Recognition of personal qualities<br>Respectful, sincere but objective tone (less intimate than that of a eulogy)<br>Acknowledgement of the deceased's survivor | ***A written communication from one person or organisation to another***<br>First-person perspective<br>Personal anecdote<br>Past tense<br>Tone<br>Grammar/punctuation<br>Structure<br>Rhetorical questions (Complaint letters)<br>Quotations<br>Facts<br>Style(s) of language (formal/colloquial, emotive)<br>Poetic devices (alliteration/symbolism/ motifs)<br>Sentence length | ***An article in a newspaper or magazine that goes into more depth than a news article and often provides comment or analysis of the factual content of the article***<br>Title/sub-title<br>Genre<br>Contention/tone<br>Point of view<br>Structure<br>Personal anecdote<br>Evidence<br>Relevant/topical examples<br>Appeals to solidarity, patriotism, fashion, vanity, fairness, tradition, modernity<br>Accompanying visuals<br>Emphatic ending |

## Stylistic Features of Visual Text Types

| MOVIE POSTER | ADVERTISEMENT / BILLBOARD | PHOTOGRAPH | CARTOON |
|---|---|---|---|
| ***A representative marketing technique used in order to create excitement and attract viewers for a film upon release***<br>Visuals<br>Genre of movie (romance, adventure, thriller, horror, etc.)<br>Caption<br>Shots/angles<br>Font (bold, size)<br>Colours<br>Names of cast, director<br>Direct addressing of viewer<br>Dramatic (melodramatic?) language<br>Sensationalism (hyperbole, emphatic punctuation) Costuming<br>Setting (foreground/ background)<br>Symbolism/motifs | ***Creates positive, differentiating, credible, relevant brand associations in consumer memory: 'the sell'***<br>Slogan<br>Logo<br>Colours<br>Symbolism/motifs<br>Font (bold, size)<br>Setting (foreground/ background)<br>Shots and angles<br>Lighting<br>Character<br>Language (subjective and objective)<br>Wardrobe<br>Positive/negative connotations<br>Contrasts<br>Imagery | ***A picture of a person or event, captured at a particular moment in time. A caption may be added in some instances to provide more information about the image***<br>Colour (or sepia/black and white)<br>Printed or digital (on screen)<br>Facial expressions<br>Setting (foreground/ background)<br>Shot (close up, mid shot etc)<br>Angle (high, low, neutral)<br>Tone of caption (if there is one)<br>Source (where is this photo displayed , e.g. blog/newspaper) | ***Combination of images and text to provide humorous viewpoint, usually with a satirical tone.***<br>Caricature (exaggeration)<br>Point of view<br>Tone<br>Positioning of figures/ objects<br>Size of figures/objects<br>Colours, shading<br>Speech bubbles<br>Caption<br>Assumed knowledge<br>Specific audience<br>Source (where is this cartoon displayed, e.g. blog/newspaper)<br>Shots and angles<br>Dialogue<br>Symbolism/motifs |

# Index of Text Types

Wakefield Press is an independent publishing and distribution company based in Adelaide, South Australia. We love good stories and publish beautiful books. To see our full range of books, please visit our website at www.wakefieldpress.com.au where all titles are available for purchase. To keep up with our latest releases, news and events, subscribe to our monthly newsletter.

Find us!

Facebook: www.facebook.com/wakefield.press
Twitter: www.twitter.com/wakefieldpress
Instagram: www.instagram.com/wakefieldpress

Printed in Australia
AUHW010536030619
312937AU00007B/7

9 781743 055755